# How to Teach Vocabulary Without Going Crazy

by Cheryl L. Callighan
illustrated by Marilynn Barr

This book is dedicated to my family
for all their loving support and patience.

Publisher: Roberta Suid
Copy Editor: Carol Whiteley
Design and Production: MGB Press
Cover Design: Dana Mardaga

ISBN1-57612-81-3
Printed in the United States of America
9 8 7 6 5 4 3 2

# CONTENTS

## PICTURESQUE SPEECH

## WORD STRUCTURE

# Introduction

Say the words "vocabulary homework" to middle schoolers and they will most likely turn pale, break out in a sweat, and feel the urge to run screaming from the room. Faced with weekly lists of words to be defined and used in sentences, most of us would react similarly. But learning vocabulary can be fun and painless when it is integrated into other areas of the curriculum.

This book provides activities that are alternatives to the traditional vocabulary-learning process of writing definitions and sentences. The lessons treat learning vocabulary as an adventure. Some of the activities incorporate games, art projects, speeches, riddles, puns, and puzzles. Other lessons keep students involved by using high-interest or unusual themes and by letting the students make choices for themselves. Several activities encourage students to stretch their imaginations and reach beyond the common, ordinary, everyday word.

Part of the trick of making the teaching and learning of vocabulary painless is to remember that vocabulary words are not limited to language arts. Vocabulary is essential in all areas of the curriculum. Each subject area has its own set of specialized words. For example, students must know the meaning of the word "trapezoid" before they can find the area of one. In science, knowing the meaning of "dilute" can significantly affect the outcome of an experiment. During a social studies unit on Egypt, learning will be greatly enhanced if students are aware that "cataract" has another meaning besides a disease that causes an opaque covering in the eye. Both you and your students will benefit if you do not view vocabulary as a singular item to be taught, but rather as a tree with multiple branches that reach into many areas.

If you teach more than one subject, be sure that you integrate each of their curriculums into your vocabulary work. Or, alternatively, be sure that you include vocabulary activities in all the curriculum areas in which you are involved. If you are a specialized language arts teacher, the key for you will be communication. Meet with the other teachers that your students see. Obtain information about the units they are currently teaching and coordinate some of your activities with theirs. If necessary, review textbooks from other subject areas in order to obtain appropriate vocabulary.

But if your class moans, groans, and rolls their eyes at the mere mention of the word "vocabulary," you may wonder why you should bother to teach vocabulary at all. There are several very important reasons. To add to an often-heard saying, you can never be too thin or too rich—or have too large a vocabulary! An increased knowledge of vocabulary words leads to greater comprehension, improved reading skills, and better communication. These in turn lead to a larger vocabulary, beginning the cycle once again.

A greater knowledge of words also builds students' confidence. It helps middle school children develop the ability to carry on conversations in a variety of social situations. It also gives the students the powerful feeling that they are acquiring adult levels of speech and can read progressively more sophisticated materials. A better and growing understanding of words additionally increases students' confidence in their writing skills as their work becomes stronger and more interesting.

It is the purpose of this book to show how a variety of activities and strategies can be used to teach vocabulary without going crazy. The book is divided into six sections:

**Management**—This section includes tips on classroom techniques, assessment, list building, and the classroom environment.

**General Activities**—The activities included may be used with teacher-generated lists or lists that have already been established.

**Creative Vocabulary Development**—These activities are designed to help students stretch their use of vocabulary words.

**Topic-Specific Vocabulary and Activities**—This section gives you a wide variety of topical vocabulary lists and specific activities to be used with each set of words.

**Picturesque Speech**—Included here are projects involving figurative language and proverbs.

**Word Structure**—This section introduces roots, and includes a lesson on acronyms and initialisms.

Teaching vocabulary should be as fluid as language itself. You will, no doubt, find favorite lessons among the various activities provided. Mixing and matching lessons will help you develop combinations that best suit your classroom. So browse, peruse, investigate, assemble, and enjoy!

# MANAGEMENT

> *Papa, potatoes, poultry, prunes and prism are all very good words for the lips, especially prunes and prism.*
>
> -Charles Dickens

## THE WORLD IN THE CLASSROOM

A wide variety of experiences is invaluable for increasing vocabulary. The more information students are exposed to, the greater possibility there is for building their knowledge of words. Bringing the world to your classroom often takes a good deal of effort on your part, but the rewards are well worth it.

Field trips, of course, are a great option for building experiences. Unfortunately, they are often costly and impractical. Instead of having one or two large trips each year, consider several smaller excursions. Look carefully at your local community—there are probably some wonderful treasures within walking distance. Close-by museums, libraries, galleries, parks, and interesting small businesses are all possibilities just waiting to be explored. Keep your eyes and ears open, and pump family and friends for information. For example, you might come across a local family whose private collection of animals rivals the natural history museum, and who would be happy to make arrangements to give your class a private tour. A little bit of digging can yield a delightful gem.

If field trips aren't possible, consider bringing the world to your classroom. Children's experiences can be enhanced by arranging to have speakers come and talk to them. Contact your local Speaker's Bureau, which acts as a clearinghouse for individuals willing to speak on a wide variety of subjects. The bureau should have a list telling you who is available and if any charge is involved. If your community does not offer such a service, consider contacting these other resources:

- Individual local businesses
- Special-interest clubs
- Local sports organizations
- City or town officials and government agencies
- Senior citizen centers or groups
- Service organizations
- The local historical society
- Nearby junior colleges, colleges, or universities
- Students' parents/relatives with interesting professions, hobbies, or skills
- Your own family and friends—and yourself; be sure to share interesting hobbies, travels, or collections.

Whenever possible, coordinate some hands-on experiences to correlate with the speakers' visits. If a weaver visits and shares her knowledge, be sure that students have the chance to attempt a simple weaving project. If a beekeeper visits, be prepared to let students have a taste of fresh honey from the hive. Don't be afraid to do something corny. If a sports figure is scheduled to speak, ask all the children to wear sport-related clothes that day. If an artist is coming to speak, cover your room with art prints borrowed from the library to create a gallery effect.

Before speakers arrive, ask them to provide you with a list of vocabulary words related to their profession or interest. Prepare the students for the visits by presenting and discussing these words. During each speaker's presentation, reinforce the vocabulary words as they are used. To culminate the experience, choose one of the general activities provided in this book and present it with the newly learned vocabulary words.

With all the experiences you plan, whether field trips or events inside the classroom, show lots of enthusiasm—your kids will be certain to catch it from you!

> *In the world of words, the imagination is one of the forces of nature.*
>
> —*Wallace Stevens*

## THE JOURNAL

A highly recommended management technique for learning vocabulary is the Vocabulary Journal, a year-long record of all vocabulary words that you want your students to be responsible for remembering. Each student should have a journal, all of which are kept in a specified location in the classroom. Students should use their journals to find words to help them with their writing. In addition, they can use the journals to collect favorite words throughout the year.

To create Vocabulary Journals, use spiral notebooks with about 70 pages of wide-rule paper. Label the journals with your students' names. Give children time to decorate and personalize their covers.

The first 50 pages of each journal should be devoted to alphabetical listings. Help the students write the letter A in the upper-right hand corner of the first page. Then have them turn this page over. Tell them to skip the next full page and look at the third page of the notebook. Have them write the letter B in the upper-right hand corner of this page. Ask the children to continue in this manner through the alphabet, allowing two pages in the journal for each letter. The letters X and Z need only one page each.

Setting up the journal may be confusing even to upper grade students. Let them take their time and make constant checks throughout the process to head off problems. Making a sample ahead of time will give the students a guide to follow. And using the sample as your own journal throughout the year will produce a master copy that children can use to help catch up after absences. Keeping your own journal will also show your willingness to learn words right along with the students.

Once the journals are prepared, illustrate the process of writing words in list fashion, followed by brief definitions. By using only one line for each word and its definition, using both the front and back of each page, the children should be able to include 100 words per letter except for X and Z.

Every vocabulary list you present during the year need not be copied into the journal. In fact, sometimes you may want to have the students enter only two or three specific words from a particular list. These would be the words the students would be responsible for knowing, while the others on the list could be used for enrichment purposes.

The journal pages following the alphabetical listings should be used to classify words by grammatical type. On these pages, have students create sections by labeling pages with the following titles. Again, each section should have at least two pages dedicated to it.

**"Noteworthy Nouns"**
**"Vivacious Verbs"**
**"Awesome Adjectives"**
**"Adventurous Adverbs"**

When the sections are labeled, tell the students that these are the pages on which they should collect their favorite words. Each time the students learn a new word that they want to use again, or simply one that intrigues them, they should write it under the correct heading. Words should also be entered after certain lessons have been presented. For example, after you work on the "Tom Swifties" exercise (see p. 63), have students add at least five new adverbs to their journals. After completing "Instead of Said" (see p. 80), students should add some verbs to their lists. Encourage your class to use words from their vocabulary journals in their writing and in their everyday conversation.

> *Proper words in proper places*
> *make the true definition of a style.*
> —Jonathan Swift

## ASSESSMENT

Testing vocabulary is optional, especially in the lower grades. Unlike spelling, which is so precise, vocabulary is more flexible; several words may be correctly used in a sentence and not greatly change the context. Learning for the sake of learning is definitely an attractive concept, and you may decide that you do not wish to impose weekly vocabulary tests on your students.

If you decide not to formally test students on all of the lists, think about rewarding them for utilizing new vocabulary words in their everyday work. Stickers could be given for using a new word in a conversation. Candy rewards (a favorite at any age) could be handed out when at least five new vocabulary words are used in a writing assignment. You might also want to consider posting a record chart that simply indicates a student's completion of the assigned activity.

If you prefer to use formal testing, a variety of testing formats can be used:

**Definition**—Provide a list of words and ask students to write the definition for each one.

**Matching**—Provide a list of words on one side of a sheet and a list of definitions on the other side. Have the students match each word to the correct definition.

**Fill-in-the-Blank**—Provide a number of sentences, each of which has a vocabulary word missing. Also provide a word bank containing all the vocabulary words. Have the students write the correct word in each blank.

**12**

**Multiple Choice**—Provide a sentence that includes each vocabulary word. Below each sentence list three different definitions. Have the students pick the definition that most correctly describes the way the word is used in the sentence.

**Phraseology**—Provide two sentences for each word.

> **For example:**
> An angle greater than 90 degrees is obscure.
> The new building will obscure our view of the lake.

Students must choose the phrase in which the vocabulary word is used correctly.

**Application**—In this type of assessment, have the students write sentences, paragraphs, or a story using a specific number of required vocabulary words. But make sure that students do not just create lists of words within sentences. Vocabulary word meaning should be apparent in the context of their writing.

> **For example:**
> Unacceptable: I saw a cowboy, a horse, some cows, and a corral.
> Acceptable: The cowboy rode his horse behind the herd of cows to steer them into the gated corral.

> *The difference between the right word and the almost right word is the difference between lightning and a lightning bug.*
>
> -Mark Twain

# BUILDING VOCABULARY LISTS

If you're a veteran teacher, you may already have a fine collection of vocabulary lists at your disposal. If you're just beginning to teach, or if you want to customize lists for your class, a wide selection of lists, plus matching activities, are available in this book. You can also refer to the following sources for additional starting points.

**Non-fiction books**—Check for a glossary. This provides an instant list of words and definitions. If the book does not contain a glossary, look in the index. There you'll find an alphabetical listing of words that are pertinent to the subject covered in the book.

**Textbooks**—Many textbooks provide a vocabulary list at the beginning of each chapter. Depending on the number of words, you can add several lists together, or pick and choose to create a custom list.

**Speakers**—Each time you invite a speaker to your classroom, be sure to ask him or her ahead of time for a list of vocabulary words that are applicable to the presentation.

**Thesaurus**—If you notice that students repeatedly use certain words, such as "happy," provide them with a list of alternatives that you find in a thesaurus: delighted, joyful, euphoric, etc.

**Word Collections**—As you read novels, magazines, and newspapers on your own, make note of interesting words in a small notebook or card file. List words alphabetically or by grammatical type.

**Discarded or Forgotten Materials**—Search through discarded spelling books, basal readers, or other old materials. Put together unusual words you find to form interesting lists.

**Previously Developed Units**—Look carefully through teaching units you developed in the past to see if you included any vocabulary lists. And as you create new units, remind yourself to develop accompanying vocabulary lists; enter new words in a notebook or card file.

**Guidelines**—Be sure to check if your state or district has established guidelines for vocabulary development.

> *Good words are worth much and cost little.*
> *-George Herbert*

## CLASSROOM ENVIRONMENT

What type of classroom environment is conducive to vocabulary development? The very same type that promotes reading and writing!

Books, books, and more books should be available in the vocabulary-promoting classroom. Be sure your selection includes plenty of variety. Non-fiction books are superb for building vocabulary—you don't have to feel that because you aren't the science teacher you can't have books about rockets, frogs, energy, or weather in your room. Even if social studies is taught down the hall, books about Egypt, China, Africa, or Colonial America should be welcome on your shelves. Cartoon books, too, including such series as <u>The Far Side,</u> <u>Foxtrot,</u> <u>Rose Is Rose,</u> <u>Calvin and Hobbes,</u> <u>Dilbert</u>, and <u>Garfield</u>, help students see how words are used in unique ways. Biographical works also often provide specialized vocabulary words that relate to the specific area of interest of the person being profiled. The vocabulary used in science fiction books is altogether different from that used to write mysteries and historical fiction.

If your space is limited, keep books boxed up in another location and rotate them through your classroom on a regular basis. Make sure that all books in the room are readily accessible to students. If you have the space, provide an inviting reading center. Middle school students enjoy being in any position that <u>doesn't</u> involve sitting upright in a chair! They love to get cozy in a squishy beanbag chair, lay under a table, drape their legs over the back of a chair, curl up in a cubicle, sit on a desk, box, or cushions, and nestle into a huge pillow. Be creative. As long as students are reading productively and not disruptive to others, their position matters little.

When it comes to writing, this is best performed while sitting upright at a desk or table. But try to build in a little relaxed time before the actual writing begins. Allow students to relax while brainstorming and creating outlines for their writing. Also encourage students to always come to class prepared with paper and pencil—but "just in case," keep extra paper and pencils on hand. It's terrible to lose a great writing idea because of a lack of writing paper.

Two books that all students must have access to in the classroom are a dictionary and a thesaurus. If your students' supply list asks them to purchase these items, be sure to specify a particular thesaurus version; various publishers have different formats, and it will make things easier if some uniformity is achieved (see the section "Creative Vocabulary Development" for some thesaurus-related lessons). You may want to require your students to bring their reference books to class every day, or you may decide to label the books and keep them on a classroom shelf. If you keep them in the room, be sure they are readily accessible whenever students need to use them.

As you work with the students, try to remember that building a good vocabulary is not done just through writing work but also through oral work. An open-minded teacher will help to promote and encourage open-ended discussions. Try to keep your discussions flexible. A discussion that begins in one area and wanders off in another direction can be extremely educational. On various occasions, arrange chairs into small groups for activities or conversations. You'll find a number of activities in this book that promote the oral side of vocabulary development.

Remember, too, that words can be fun. To promote this aspect,

**16**

provide an area where students may spend optional time—any place from an elaborate, complete learning center to a table with a folder and a shoebox of materials. Load the area with crossword puzzles, anagrams, cryptoquizzes, and search-a-word puzzles; check garage sales for old word-game puzzle magazines and newspapers that include word puzzles for children. Games such as <u>Scrabble, Upwords,</u> and <u>Boggle</u> will encourage students to stretch their word-recall abilities. Also encourage students to create their own word games or puzzles to add to the center. If you are lucky enough to have a computer in your room, think about providing some of the games that are available on software.

As you consider your classroom environment, remember to think about what goes up on your walls. Middle school students enjoy a physically attractive environment. Interesting photographs or reprints of classical art may inspire a whole list of new vocabulary words. Posters may contain phrases or sentiments that will broaden students' horizons. Use what you have available and try to look at the pieces in different ways. A favorite poster could turn out to be a great springboard for a creative writing assignment.

# BULLETIN BOARDS

If you have bulletin boards throughout your room, don't despair. Make one work for your vocabulary lessons. Create a background that you keep up throughout the school year. Then give different students the task (to some it may be a reward) of changing the temporary parts of the board to match the current vocabulary lesson. A number of bulletin board ideas follow that involve a permanent background and student involvement.

## The Tree

For the permanent background—Cover the top three-fourths of the bulletin board surface with light blue paper. Cover the bottom quarter with green paper. Cut the top edge of the green paper, where it meets the blue paper, unevenly so that it simulates grass. Across the top of the display place cut-out letters that spell "Watch Our Vocabulary Grow!" Use brown paper to create a tree trunk and several large branches. If you'd like a three-dimensional effect, twist the large-branch paper into ropes and staple them to the board. Draw in smaller branches with a brown marker.

To use throughout the year, choose one or several of the following options and let students change and maintain the board.

**Option 1:** Cut out a number of green leaf shapes. Write one vocabulary word on each shape and staple to the smaller tree branches. To update the display simply remove the leaves and replace with a new set.

**Option 2:** Do not remove any leaf shapes. Simply continue adding leaves to fill up all the branches.

**Option 3:** During the fall, use red, yellow, and orange leaves or hang apple shapes from the branches.

**Option 4:** In the winter, consider hanging snowflakes or icicle shapes on the tree.

**Option 5:** Create simple blossom shapes in pink, purple, white, or yellow to add to the tree in the springtime. Or have the children cut out brightly colored bird shapes. Write a vocabulary word on each shape and attach all to the display so that it looks as if the birds are sitting on the branches. Students might also design some nests or birdhouses on which to write vocabulary words, and place them among the tree branches.

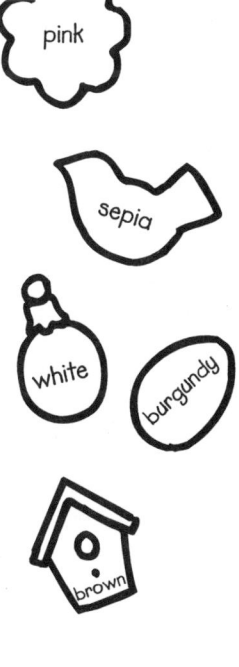

# Watch Our Vocabulary Grow

# Watch Our Vocabulary Grow

Leaves: burgundy, bronze, teal, beige, gold, orange, olive, coral, blue, brown, sepia, silver, khaki, magenta, amber, copper, purple, lavender, white, plum, red, pink, green, black, gray, tan

# Watch Our Vocabulary Grow

Birds: eagle, crow, ostrich, wren, tern, pheasant, sparrow, robin, turkey, egret, bluebird, hawk, thrush, duck, partridge, goose, cardinal, canary, peacock, pigeon, dove

# Magnifying Glass

For the permanent background—Cover the entire bulletin board in a light color, preferably white. At the very top, place cut-out letters that spell "Focus on. . ." Create a three-dimensional magnifying glass handle with the cardboard tube from a roll of gift wrap. Paint the tube black and attach it to the board at an angle on the far left of the display. Cut out a thin strip of gray or silver poster board to form the circle of the lens. Cover the circle with a piece of thin, clear plastic (a recycled dry cleaner's bag or thin plastic drop cloth works well), taping it in place. Carefully staple the circle to the bulletin board to form the magnifying glass.

To use throughout the year, choose one or several of the following options and let students change and maintain the board.

**Option 1:** To the right of the lens, place cut-out letters that spell "Sports." Directly below this, staple a page from the sports section of the newspaper. Cut out 20 small rectangles from colored paper or use index cards. Referring to the vocabulary list for "Sports" on p. 92, write one word on each rectangle. Staple these rectangles randomly over the newspaper page.

**Option 2:** To the right of the lens place cut-out letters that spell "Outdoor Adventure." Below this staple a variety of scenic outdoor pictures from magazines or old calendars. On a sheet of colored paper, write the vocabulary words from the "Outdoor Adventure" list found on p. 88. Staple this list in the middle of the scenic photographs.

**Option 3:** To the right of the lens place cut-out letters that spell "Compounds." Create several sets of picture codes depicting compound words similar to the activity listed under "Compounds" (see p. 84). Have these picture codes illustrate words that are not on the list, and use them to introduce the activity to the students. When the students have completed their picture codes, add as many of these to the display as possible.

**Option 4:** For this display you will need several old road maps or an old road atlas that you don't mind cutting apart. From one of the maps cut out letters that spell "The Route Stuff" and staple them to the right of the magnifying glass. Below this title staple one or more maps. On a sheet of colored paper, write vocabulary words you choose from the "On the Road" list (see p. 81).

**Option 5:** From old newspaper cut out the letters to spell "Newspapers" and place them to the right of the lens. On the left side of the remaining space, on a sheet of colored paper, print the vocabulary words you choose from the lesson entitled "The Newspaper" (see p. 95). To the right of them staple several newspaper pages or sections. With pins and yarn, connect some of the vocabulary words to the related items in the newspaper. For example, pin one end of a piece of yarn to the word "headline" and pin the other end to an actual headline. You won't be able to do this for every word, but matching five to seven terms and items will make for an interesting bulletin board.

# FOCUS ON...

# FOCUS ON...
## compounds

     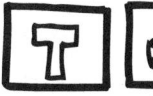   

# FOCUS ON...
## NEWSPAPERS

 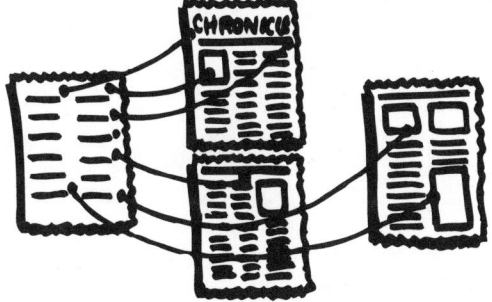

# Hot Air Balloon

For the permanent background—Cover the entire board with pale blue paper. From brightly colored paper, cut a large circle (adjusting it to the size of the board) to form the hot air balloon. Add stripes, polka dots, stars, or other decorations to the balloon if you like. Staple the balloon to the bulletin board (attaching it slightly off center will allow you to make use of more options), allowing plenty of room on both sides to add to the display. From brown paper, cut a square to represent the basket. Round off the corners and attach it directly below the balloon. Connect the basket to the balloon by stapling four equal-length pieces of string or yarn to the top of the basket. Staple the other ends of the yarn to the balloon. Using cut-out letters, add the title "Reach New Heights."

To use throughout the year, choose one or several of the following options and let students change and maintain the board.

**Option 1:** Cut out three or four large white clouds. Write several vocabulary words on each cloud and place them in the blue sky.

**Option 2:** Cut out a large yellow sun and place it in the blue sky. Cut out 20 small orange triangles. Write one vocabulary word on each triangle and attach them to form the rays of the sun. (Or attach the rays first before writing the words so that you avoid having some words read upside down.)

**Option 3:** Let each student draw and cut out a bird shape. Write one vocabulary word on each bird. (If you have more birds than words, write review vocabulary from previous lessons on some of the birds). Attach the birds to the background.

replied
whispered
cried yelled
answered
moaned

asked
screamed
questioned fussed
mumbled squealed
announced

exclaimed
commented informed
babbled complained
implored reminded

# Computer

This is a very simple display and best used on a small, square bulletin board. As you cut out the shapes to create the computer, keep in mind that you want the computer to fill up most of the bulletin board.

Start by covering the background with a bright color. If you have access to a computer graphics program, print out a banner to read "Get Online with These Words." Or create a banner by hand or with stencils.

To create the monitor, cut out a large white rectangle. Cut out a slightly smaller green or blue rectangle to be the screen. Staple the white rectangle to the bulletin board first, then staple the green rectangle on top of it. Cut out a thin white trapezoid to staple on below the monitor to represent the base. Cut out and staple on a larger white trapezoid for the keyboard. On the keyboard draw a number of squares and rectangles to represent the various keys. Don't worry about trying to be precise.

To use throughout the year, choose one or both of the following options and let students change and maintain the board.

**Option 1:** Cut out a whole stack of green or blue "screens." Then simply write the week's vocabulary words on a screen and staple it to the monitor.

**Option 2:** Use a word processing program that offers various fonts. Each time you type up a vocabulary list to post on the screen, make sure you create it in a different font.

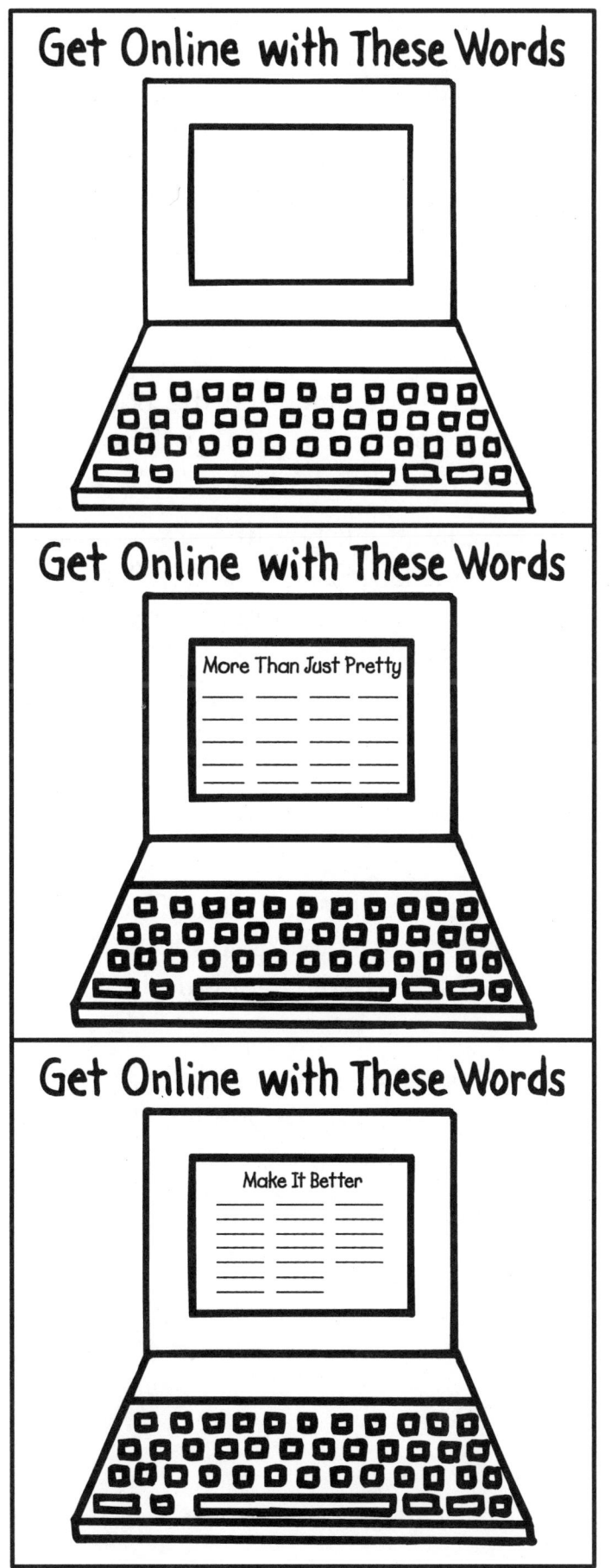

**Get Online with These Words**

**Get Online with These Words**

More Than Just Pretty

**Get Online with These Words**

Make It Better

# The Gift

For the permanent background—Cover the bulletin board with bright wrapping paper (be sure any pattern is age appropriate). Choose one color that is found in the design and cut out two thin strips of paper in that color. Crisscross the strips on the board so that they look like ribbon. To create a bow for the top of the package, lay out four thin strips of paper as if they were spokes in a wheel. Staple them together in the very center. Carefully bring up each end, bending it toward the center, and staple it to the center. Add the bow to the display. Use cut-out letters to title the display "The Gift of Words."

Next, take the top of a large gift box (the size used for a shirt or sweater) and staple the largest surface area flat against the background. This area will act as a "frame" for your list of words. Take several other smaller box tops or bottoms, the deeper the better, and staple in the same manner on other parts of the display. These boxes will serve as frames or shadowboxes for small items that correlate to your word list. Use your imagination to come up with pictures or small items to fill the boxes.

**Option 1:** Write the list from the lesson called "Zoo" (see p. 89) on bright colored paper and staple it inside the largest box. Place small plastic or stuffed animals inside the smaller shadowboxes.

**Option 2:** Using a large sheet of sandpaper and a dark colored crayon or pencil write the vocabulary list entitled "Seashore" (see p. 94). Place this list inside the largest box. Decorate the smaller boxes with shells, rocks, or pieces of driftwood.

How to Teach Vocabulary Without Going Crazy • ©1999 Monday Morning Books

# The Gift
# of Words

# The Gift
# of Words

Seashore

# The Gift
# of Words

ZOO

# GENERAL ACTIVITIES

The following pages provide activities that can be used with preestablished, teacher-generated vocabulary lists. The following section, Creative Vocabulary Development, contains lessons that ask students to be responsible for word development, encouraging both creativity and vocabulary enhancement.

Some of the activities in this section can be described as "word play," helping the children become more familiar with words themselves. Other lessons focus on providing a unique experience as well as words to describe that experience. All of the activities will add to a student's experiential background, leading to increased vocabulary, better comprehension and communication, and wider experiences, in a never-ending cycle.

# Concentration

An extremely useful tool for building vocabulary is the game of Concentration. The game board needed here takes some effort to create, but once completed it can be used year after year.

## Materials:

Piece of foam board or heavy cardboard, 40 card pockets (the type used by libraries) or 40 squares of heavy paper, index cards, glue, scissors, markers, stickers (optional), vocabulary list

## Preparation:

1. Lay out the 40 pockets on the piece of foam board in an orderly grid pattern (five rows of eight pockets each is recommended).

2. Carefully glue each pocket to the board. If you are using paper squares, glue only three edges to the board, leaving the top edge unglued to form a pocket.

3. Use a dark-colored marker to number the pockets 1 through 40.

4. Add the title "Concentration" to the top of the game board. If desired, decorate the board with markers and colorful stickers.

5. Cut 20 index cards in half. Write each vocabulary word on one half of a card. Write the definition on the other half.

6. Thoroughly mix up the cards. Place one card half in each pocket on the game board. Be sure that you have the backs of the cards facing outward so that no writing is visible.

## Activity:

1. Divide the class into two teams (Red and Blue are used here for easy reference).

2. Explain to the class that the object of the game is to match each vocabulary word with its definition. To do this players must call out two numbers at a time and hope for a match. Remind students that it takes "concentration" to remember where certain words and definitions are located. Students must think for themselves. Any team member shouting out a number or a clue to another player will cause the team to lose a turn. Point out that students must pay attention to the game play at all times in order to discover and remember correct matches.

3. Begin by having the first player on the Red team call out a number. Pull out the card from that number pocket and read it aloud to the class. Then have the same player guess a second number and read the card from that pocket. Ask the student whether or not the cards match a vocabulary word with its definition.

4. If the two cards match (word and definition), the Red team scores a point and the cards are removed from the game. The Red team player takes another turn.

5. If the cards do not match, they are returned to their respective pockets. The Blue team then has its turn.

6. Play continues in this manner until all the matches have been made.

# Memory

This game is very similar to Concentration, but does not require the construction of a game board. It is designed to be played in groups of two to four players.

**Materials:**
Index cards (20 cards for each group of students participating), markers, scissors, vocabulary list

**Preparation:**
1. Cut the index cards in half.

2. Using a marker, write a vocabulary word on one half of each card and the definition on the other half.

**Activity:**
1. Divide the class into small groups of two-four players. (If you are not planning to have the whole class participate, use a learning center concept. Place the cards and instructions in an area where a group of students may play the game.) Tell the students that the object of the game is to make the most correct matches of word and definition.

2. Shuffle the cards and lay them out on a table face down. Once the cards have been placed, they should not be moved around.

3. The first player turns over two cards. If the cards match (correct word and definition), that player keeps the two cards and takes another turn.

4. If the cards do not match, they are returned to their original positions and play moves to the next player.

5. Play continues until all the cards have been correctly matched.

# Television Guide Summaries

A format familiar to students—television program summaries—encourages students to be creative.

**Materials:**

Television listing guides from newspapers or magazines (be sure program descriptions are included, not just broadcasting times), vocabulary list, paper, pencils

**Activity:**

1. Begin the activity by reading several sample listings. Remind students that these summaries provide very brief descriptions of TV programs that will be aired.

2. Tell the students that they are going to create similar program listings using their vocabulary words. They are to write one program summary for each of their words.

3. Have the students come up with several names of television programs. If desired, they may also come up with movie titles and include movie summaries as part of their listings.

4. Ask the students to write the names of their programs followed by the summary of the episode or plot. Be sure to have them underline the vocabulary word they use in each listing.

> **Example:**
> I Dream of Jeannie—Jeannie blinks Major Nelson to a desert <u>island</u>.
>
> Bewitched—Endora turns Darrin into a mule at the bottom of a <u>canyon</u>.

5. If possible, take the time to have students read aloud three or four of their favorite entries.

# Telephone Game

This activity promotes writing, verbal, listening, and group skills all in one lesson. The game tends to get a little noisy, but it is a fun end-of-the-week review.

**Materials:**
Vocabulary list, paper, pencils

**Activity:**
1. Tell the students that they are going to play an old-fashioned party game. To prepare for the game, they must first write a brief definition for each of their vocabulary words.

2. Once all the students have their lists of definitions, divide the class into two or three groups. (The game can be played as a whole class, but fewer definitions will be covered and children will tend to lose interest faster.)

3. Have each group sit in a circle. One person in each group is the operator. The operator whispers the definition of a word in the ear of the person to his or her right. This student, in turn, whispers the definition in the ear of the next person. The "message" is passed all the way around the circle until it reaches the person seated on the operator's left. That person then announces what he or she heard. Chances are the definition will have changed significantly as it was passed around the circle.

4. The operator then reads the correct definition that was given as the original message.

5. The student sitting on the operator's right becomes the new operator. He or she starts another message on its way around the circle.

6. Play continues as long as time allows.

# What It Is!

This exercise has a flexible format and can be used with any vocabulary list or number of words. A valuable option is to use a "Word of the Day" concept. Each day one word is chosen by the teacher or a student and presented and explored using this format.

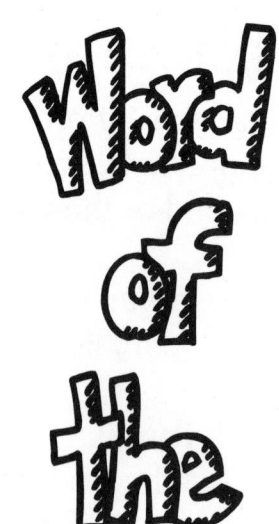

## Materials:

Poster board, markers, overhead projector or chalkboard, vocabulary list

## Preparation:

Create a poster that includes the headings shown below in bold type. The poster should list just the headings—the comments are added here for your information. The headings will act as a guide for the students to follow when presenting a "Word of the Day" or when writing up words in a vocabulary list.

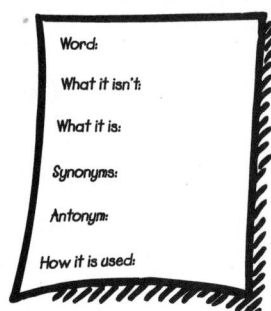

**Word:** Write the featured word.

**What it isn't:** Remarkably, answering this often helps students remember a word more than any other strategy. It also provides the opportunity for students to work on beginning skills in word origin and meanings of suffixes and prefixes. Allow students to make this definition plausible or humorous.

**What it is:** Write the definition of the word.

**Synonyms:** One or more synonyms should be listed.

**Antonym:** If applicable, the student should list an antonym. If not applicable, the student should write "none," "nil," "zero," or "void where prohibited."

**How it is used:** A sentence should be given that clearly indicates the meaning of the word.

**Activity:**

1. If you are using the activity with the Word of the Day format, the student responsible should come to class with the information prepared. You may have the student give the report orally or write it on the chalkboard or overhead. Remind students that they should always follow the format.

2. If you are using the activity with a list of words, it is best to have the students present their information in written form. Their papers should include the headings listed above for each word.

> The word is subtraction. It is not the active dislike of subway tracks.

**Example:**

**Word:** subtraction

**What it isn't:** the active dislike of subway tracks

**What it is:** the act of removing numbers or objects from a given set; a mathematical operation

**Synonyms:** minus, removal, reduction

**Antonym:** addition

**How it is used:** We will reduce the large number by using subtraction.

**Option:** Another way of using this format is to create worksheets that list the headings, followed by blank spaces. When you have a specific word you want the students to remember, fill out a worksheet for that word together as a class. Keep the worksheets in a notebook to develop a file of vocabulary words for your classroom.

# Flipbooks

This activity acts as a review to help students practice matching vocabulary words to their meanings.

**Materials:**
Small spiral notebooks of blank index cards, vocabulary words and definitions, markers, scissors or paper cutter

**Preparation:**
1. Cut the notebook cards in half from top to bottom leaving the spiral wire intact. This can be done with a paper cutter after a little practice and with a lot of care.

2. On the left half of each index card, write the desired vocabulary word.

3. On the right half of each card, write the definition for another word so that words and definitions are not directly across from each other.

4. Code the correct answers in the following manner. Flip the notebook pages until you match word and definition. Carefully turn these pages to their backs. Using a marker, draw a colored symbol on each half that will match up when the two halves meet. Be sure to make each symbol a different style or color to avoid confusion.

**Activity:**
1. Give the student the flipbook. Have him or her begin by reading each of the vocabulary words, then each of the definitions.

2. Tell the student to match each word to the correct definition.

3. Once the student thinks a match has been made, have him or her look at the back of the two halves. If the symbols on both halves match, the answer is correct.

# Puzzle Pairs

Students make word/definition puzzles to challenge their friends.

**Materials:**
Colored paper, markers or crayons, envelopes, paper cutter, scissors, vocabulary list

**Preparation:**
Using a paper cutter, cut rectangles of colored paper. You will need enough rectangles for each student to have one for each word on the vocabulary list.

**Activity:**
1. Give each student the needed number of rectangles. Tell the children that they are going to create puzzle pairs.

2. On the left side of each rectangle, students should write a vocabulary word. On the right side, they should write the word's definition or synonym.

3. Once they have completed the writing, the students should cut the rectangles in half between the word and the definition. Be sure that they make a squiggly line and not just a straight cut. If the students want to make their puzzles more difficult, they should make the identical cut on every rectangle. They may accomplish this by first cutting a pattern piece from a separate rectangle and then tracing it on to their puzzle rectangles.

4. Have students place their completed puzzle pairs in an envelope and write their name on it. They may decorate the envelope if they like.

5. Divide the class into pairs. Have the students exchange puzzle pieces with their partner and reassemble all the puzzle pairs.

# Language Olympics Part I

This activity involves three short challenges that you can relate to an Olympics theme. You may award a gold, silver, and bronze medal to the top three performers in each event, or gold, silver, and bronze (or other color) star stickers. Enhance the theme by allowing students to choose a country to represent. Let the children draw that country's flag and tape it to their desks. Because children at this age are very competitive, you may want to hold several Language Olympics throughout the year. This will give students a chance to see how they are progressing in their abilities.

**Materials:**

Paper and pencils, prepared worksheets

**Preparation:**

1. You will need to create two different short worksheets for the challenges; each worksheet can fit on a half sheet of paper. However, don't put both challenges on the same sheet since these are timed events and it wouldn't be fair to have a preview of the coming challenge. Using the front and back side of a paper won't work either, since you should pass out all of the papers face down in order to keep the timed part of the challenge fair.

2. On a half sheet of paper, scramble each of the vocabulary words. Leave a space next to each anagram for the correct word to be written.

3. On another half sheet of paper, write a synonym or brief clue to serve as a definition for each vocabulary word.

**Activity:**

1. Remind the students about the spirit of the Olympics. Tell them that many of the athletes compete to better their performances as well as to win medals. Encourage students to try their best in each event.

2. Hold the "Scramble Challenge" event. Pass out the worksheets containing the anagrams. Be sure to place them face down on the students' desks. Tell the students they will have exactly five minutes (or the time that's appropriate for your students) to attempt to unscramble all the words. Say "Go!" and start timing. At the end of the allotted time, call out "Stop!" To determine the event's top three finishers, count the number of correct answers on each student's paper.

3. Hold the "Long Jump" event. Begin by telling the students that they are being challenged to write the longest sentence using as many vocabulary words as possible. The rules are:

- The sentence must make sense and be understandable.
- The sentence must begin with a capital letter.
- The sentence must contain all proper punctuation.

Give the students paper and pencils and five minutes to complete this challenge. At the end of the time limit, have students count the number of vocabulary words in their sentence. Have all the students with the highest number of words stand in order in the front of the room. Check each sentence to be sure it meets the criteria. Eliminate those that have not been correctly written. Declare the top three winners in the event.

4. Hold the event "Synonym Slalom." Pass out the worksheets containing the synonyms and clue words. Be sure that you place them face down on the desks. Tell the students that they are to match each of the vocabulary words to one of the synonyms. Give them only two minutes to complete this task. Time the students and, at the end of the challenge, determine the winners.

5. It is very possible that some of the challenges will result in ties. At the beginning of the year it would be appropriate to award prizes to all the winners. But near the end of the year it may be fun to hold some tough tie breakers. One possible tie breaker is to call out a letter. Students then have 30 seconds to write as many vocabulary words as they can that contain that letter.

# Picture File Fun

A picture file is an invaluable asset at any grade level. To make one, collect photographs and drawings from magazines, calendars, catalogues, travel brochures, and small posters. Then use the pictures to encourage creative writing and vocabulary development.

**Materials:**
A wide variety of pictures, vocabulary list, paper and pencils, thesaurus (optional for some activities)

**Activities** (choose one or more of the following):
1. Pass out one picture to each student. Have the children look carefully at their picture and then look at the vocabulary list. Have the students write down any word from the list that could apply to their particular picture. Encourage students to really stretch their imaginations.

> **Example:**
> The photograph depicts an African landscape. A lion is in the foreground. There are trees in the distance and dark clouds behind them. The vocabulary word "scenic" might apply. The student's sentence: "The lion is sleeping in the <u>scenic</u> landscape."

Remind students that they must be able to give a plausible explanation for their choices. Be sure students underline the vocabulary words.

2. Have students write sentences that use a vocabulary word in each one. The sentences should directly relate to their pictures in some manner. Unlike the previous activity, the sentences do not have to describe just the picture; they may also describe the students' feelings about the pictures. Using the same photograph described above, a student might write :

> I would be very <u>grateful</u> if I could visit Africa.

Remind students that they should underline the vocabulary word used in each sentence.

How to Teach Vocabulary Without Going Crazy • ©1999 Monday Morning Books

3. Divide the class into groups of two or three. Across the front of the room display ten pictures. Have each group of students choose one picture, but not tell which one they chose. If desired, you might number the pictures and then secretly assign one to each group in order to assure variety. Tell the groups to come up with three or four sentences that describe their chosen picture. Each sentence must include a vocabulary word. Then, have the students share their descriptive sentences. Let the rest of the class guess which picture each group is describing.

4. Select ten pictures and number them from 1 through 10. Display the pictures so that all the students can view them. Have the students look at the pictures and think about the mood in each one.

> **Examples:**
> 1. The photograph depicts a girl holding a kitten. The mood for this picture might be peaceful, calm, or enchanting.
>
> 2. The photograph shows a family that is poverty stricken. The mood for this might be described as depressing, hopeless, or oppressive.

Next, have the students number their papers 1 through 10. Ask them to try to come up with at least three words to describe the mood in each photograph. Remind the class that the thesaurus is a valuable tool for this exercise. Once they have thought of at least one descriptive word, they may use the thesaurus to find several more.

# You Make the Challenge

Here students create the activity by developing and then completing each other's worksheets.

**Materials:**

Paper and pencils, dictionary and thesaurus (one for each student), rulers, graph paper, vocabulary list

**Activity:**

1. Tell the students that they are each going to develop an interesting worksheet to challenge another classmate.

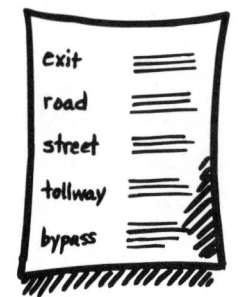

2. Review the vocabulary list. Remind students that all the vocabulary words on the list must be used in creating their worksheets.

3. Give the students a list of options to choose from for their worksheets. Instruct students to write carefully and clearly so that their classmates will be able to read and understand the pages. Each challenge paper should include at least three different types of activities. Several possibilities follow, and students should also be encouraged to develop other games or puzzles that would work well with their vocabulary words.

> • **Fill in the blank**—Students write a sentence that includes a vocabulary word, but leave the space for it blank.
> • **Scramble**—The letters of a vocabulary word are scrambled, and the challenge is to unscramble the word.
> • **Synonym Match**—The challenge is to match two or three synonyms to the correct vocabulary word.
> • **Search a Word**—Students design a word search puzzle on graph paper.
> • **Code Words**—Students develop a code, write it down, and then write each of the vocabulary words in code. The challenge is to decode the words.
> • **Matching**—Students write a list of definitions and then challenge their classmates to match the correct vocabulary word to each definition.

4. After the challenge worksheets have been created, collect them and redistribute for students to complete.

How to Teach Vocabulary Without Going Crazy • ©1999 Monday Morning Books

# Paint Blots

Spots of tempera paint make interesting shapes that inspire students to be creative.

**Materials:**

White or manila drawing paper, tempera paint (more than one color makes it more fun), small plastic spoons, paper and pencils, scissors, newspaper, vocabulary list

**Preparation:**

1. Cut the paper into small squares. Make enough squares to give two to each child.

2. Prepare a work area. Cover the surface with newspaper.

**Activity:**

1. Let students use the spoons to put a very few drops of tempera paint in the center of a square. The closer the drops are to the center, the better the result will be. After the drops are in place, have the students fold the paper and gently press it, rubbing from the fold outward. Then have them unfold the paper, enjoy the result, and set it aside to dry. Most likely the children will be so fascinated by this process that they will want to create a second blot.

2. After the blots have dried, number each one for reference. Place them on display around the room. Discuss how some of the paint blots remind you of certain shapes, images, moods, or objects. Point out that each student may interpret a blot in his or her own unique way. Turn several of the blots to show that the perceived image may change as its position is shifted.

3. Ask the students to each choose ten blots. Have them write the numbers of these blots on their papers.

4. Tell the class that they are to come up with a title or descriptive phrase for each of the blots they have chosen. Each title must include one of their vocabulary words. Also have the students write one or two sentences explaining why they chose the particular title for each blot.

# Mini-Book Clubs

Use this activity when the vocabulary list comes directly from a novel or story the class is reading.

**Materials:**
Paper and pencils, vocabulary list, specific reading material, discussion questions

**Preparation:**
Prepare a list of questions, based on the reading selection, for the book clubs to use during their discussions.

**Activity:**
1. Divide the class into small groups of four or five. Try to arrange for the groups to meet in separate areas.

2. Have each student bring the reading selection, discussion questions, list of vocabulary words, and a pencil to the group.

3. Tell students that they will be discussing the reading selection. As they talk, they should tally the number of times they hear one of the vocabulary words used. Have the students answer the questions you have prepared, reading aloud the passages that substantiate their responses. If a vocabulary word is read, the students should add another tally mark.

4. If it is too difficult or distracting for each student to keep a tally, try assigning a group secretary. This person would keep the tally for the entire group. If a group secretary is used, assign a second one halfway through the discussion. Depending on the abilities of your class you might also want to assign a discussion leader for each group. This person would be responsible for asking the discussion questions and for keeping the discussion on track.

5. Just for fun, serve refreshments during the book club sessions.

# International Symbols

Commonplace international symbols help students *see* vocabulary words in a new light.

## Materials:

Drawing paper, markers, rulers, pencils, international symbol images, vocabulary list

## Preparation:

To do this activity you will need to gather some images of international symbols. Common ones are the blue and white H for hospital, the plane silhouette that indicates an airport, and the green and white P for parking. Many international symbols are available as computer clip art. "Rules of the Road" books also contain many of these signs and are available at no charge from your local Department of Motor Vehicles.

## Activity:

1. Show the class some samples of international symbols. Point out that even if you did not speak the language of the country where such a sign was posted you would be able to understand what the sign meant. Ask the students to think of as many of these symbols as they can. For example, if they used a public washroom lately they may have noticed the figures indicating "Men" and "Women." Make the students aware that most international symbols are usually presented in only two colors, usually a color and white, and that the images are portrayed in silhouette fashion. The symbols are very simple with very little detail. Also point out that almost all of the symbols are placed in a square.

2. Tell the students that they are going to come up with an international symbol to represent each of their vocabulary words.

3. Give each child a sheet of drawing paper and a ruler. Have the students use the rulers to make the required number of squares on their paper. Let the students use the markers to create vocabulary symbols. Remind students to write each vocabulary word under its corresponding image.

# Pass Along

This cooperative challenge helps students write complex sentences.

**Materials:**
Paper and pencils, vocabulary list

**Preparation:**
This activity works best if you utilize several vocabulary lists. If you have been using the journal method (see p. 10), then students should have their journals on their desks. If you have not used journals, then make up a list of vocabulary words that you want the students to use.

**Activity:**
1. Review the vocabulary words that you will be using during this lesson. Make sure that the class remembers the definition for each word.

2. Take a few minutes to remind students about proper sentence punctuation.

3. Explain to the class that they will be working cooperatively. They will be creating complex sentences by passing sentence fragments around the room.

4. Have everyone begin with one piece of paper on his or her desk. In the first round, each student should write a simple phrase using one of the vocabulary words. This phrase should not be a complete sentence, but should begin with a capital letter and have the context of the beginning of a sentence. Tell the students to underline the vocabulary word used in the phrase.

5. In round two, each person passes his or her paper to another student. Students now add a second phrase—again containing a vocabulary word—to the beginning of the sentence. Remind students that the vocabulary word in the second phrase should be underlined.

6. For round three, have the students pass the papers once more. This time, each student completes the sentence received with a phrase that includes another vocabulary word. After students add the third-round phrase they are responsible for checking the sentence to be sure it is complete and that all punctuation is included and correct.

Here are two examples of how sentences might look as they are progressing through the rounds.

The zookeeper explained the tremendous benefits of the new reptile habitat.

Round 1    I will <u>create</u>
Round 2    I will <u>create</u> a new, <u>superb</u>
Round 3    I will <u>create</u> a new, <u>superb</u> recipe for <u>delectable</u> chocolate.

Round 1    The <u>zookeeper</u>
Round 2    The <u>zookeeper</u> explained the <u>tremendous</u> benefits
Round 3    The <u>zookeeper</u> explained the <u>tremendous</u> benefits of the new reptile <u>habitat</u>.

7. When the sentences are complete and checked, take a few minutes to have students read aloud some of the sentences that have been written.

8. Tell the class to skip a line on their papers and begin another "pass along" sentence. Continue the three-round process for as long as desired.

# Communication Game

Charades, Pictionary, and Password—all rolled into one.

**Materials:**
Dice, index cards, one-minute timers, paper and pencils (you can use the backs of old worksheets), scissors, vocabulary list

**Preparation:**
1. Make a game kit for each group playing. A kit consists of:

> Word Cards        Communication Chart
> One-minute timer     A die
> Drawing paper and a pencil

2. To make the Word Cards, cut the index cards in thirds. Write one of the vocabulary words on each small card. The game works well if you have a wide variety of words.

3. Use a whole index card to make a Communication Chart for each kit. On each chart write the following:

> 1 or 2 ACT       3 or 4 DRAW       5 or 6 EXPLAIN

**Activity:**
1. Divide the class into groups of four to six students.

2. Place each group's Communication Chart where all players can see it. Stack the Word Cards face down in the center of the group. Have the students decide who will go first by rolling the die. The player with the highest number goes first.

3. Explain the rules of the game, which follow.

> To begin play, the player rolls the die and checks the Communication Chart. If the player rolled a 1 or 2, he or she must ACT out the word that will be chosen; a 3 or 4 means the word must be DRAWN; and a 5 or 6 means the word must be EXPLAINED. Once the action is determined, the player takes the top card from the Word Card pile. The timer is turned over and the player has one minute to communicate the word, following the rules.

# Communication Chart

**ACT**—The acting must be strictly non-verbal; no sounds and no drawing are allowed. The player may use objects around the room as props. If the Word Card contains a phrase, the player may indicate to the group the number of words and which part of a word or phrase is currently being acted out.

**DRAW**—The player must be completely silent as he or she draws. Nodding or pointing is allowed to indicate when part of the word or answer has been correctly guessed. Numbers and words may NOT be used in the drawing. A player may break the word down into component parts and draw these separately.

**EXPLAIN**—This form of communication must be strictly verbal. However, words related to or derived from the vocabulary word may NOT be used. For example, if the word is successful, the player may not use the phrase "what you become if you succeed." Hand and other body motions are NOT allowed.

### Scoring

Players earn one point for each word they are able to successfully communicate in one minute or less.

# Character Dialogues

Writing an imagined conversation between two famous characters or people is a great way to use and expand vocabulary.

**Materials:**

Paper and pencils, vocabulary list

**Activity:**

1. Review the format for writing dialogue. If each speaker's name is followed by a colon, no quotation marks are required around the words to be spoken. Remind students to start a new line each time a different character speaks.

2. Have students choose two favorite characters. They could be characters who are found together, such as Batman and Robin, Romeo and Juliet, or Tom and Jerry. Or they could be unlikely pairs, such as the Queen of England and Michael Jordan, Mickey Mouse and Abraham Lincoln, or Cinderella and Aladdin, who are likely to produce unusual dialogue.

3. Once the students have chosen their characters, tell them to write a conversation between the two using all of the vocabulary words. Remind students to underline each vocabulary word as it is used in the dialogue. Here is a short example:

> **James Bond:** Hello, Q. Have you been feeling <u>creative?</u>
>
> **Q:** Yes, James. Here is a very <u>innovative</u> item.
>
> **James:** I hope it does something <u>destructive!</u>
>
> **Q:** Actually, it is very <u>constructive.</u> I call it Instant Bridge.

# CREATIVE VOCABULARY DEVELOPMENT

## Language Olympics Part II

These activities differ from the original Language Olympics (see p. 40) in that no vocabulary list is used with the challenges. Students must call on their own knowledge of words in order to compete in each event.

**Materials:**
Overhead or chalkboard, paper and pencils, five interesting objects (stuffed toy, vase, apple, flower, globe, clothing item, telephone, science model, etc.)

**Preparation:**
Have in mind a 10-, 11-, or 12-letter word that contains a lot of common letters. Possibilities: grandmother, skateboard, strawberries, apartments, rollerblades, intelligent, encyclopedia, birdhouses.

**Activity:**
1. Remind the students that in the Olympics the major emphasis is on participation and personal achievement. Encourage all students to try their very best. Also tell the students that none of these events allows for an instant announcement of the winners. Papers must be checked over and scores tallied, so winners will be declared at a later time.

2. Hold the "Paragraph Marathon." Tell students that they are to write a paragraph about any subject that they choose. The challenge here is that no word in the paragraph may contain the letters m, r, or t (or any other combination of common consonants). The paragraph must make sense and the sentences must have a subject and a verb. Give the students 15 minutes to complete the task. You will need to check the paragraphs for accuracy. Determine the winner by first determining those students who have completed the most correct sentences. Then count the number of words in the correct sentences. Award prizes to the three students who used the highest number of words.

3. Hold the Super Word Challenge. On the overhead or chalkboard, write the letters of the long word you selected to use. Write the word in the following manner: vowels first in alphabetical order, then consonants in alphabetical order. If you selected grandmother, you would write the letters in this manner: a e o d g h m n r r t. Tell the students that they are to use the letters to form as many words as possible that meet the following rules:

- Each word must be four or more letters long.
- Each word must be spelled correctly to be counted in the final score.
- No foreign words, slang, abbreviations, or proper nouns are allowed.
- If an s is one of the letters, then plurals are acceptable.
- In order to be considered as a prize winner, students must include a super word (one word using all the letters) in their list.
- All words must be formed within 20 minutes.

At the end of the 20-minute time period, have students circle the word that includes every letter. If they did not come up with one of these words, they are eliminated from the competition. Collect all the papers and check the words to be sure all meet the criteria. Cross out any words that are incorrect. Count the number of correct words. The winners are those students who have the three highest numbers of correct words.

4. Hold the Adjective Dash. Display the five items you have chosen to use for this event. Give students a few minutes to look over the objects. Tell them that they should each choose one item. Distribute paper to the students and have them place their pencils on the floor. Tell the students that they are to come up with as many adjectives as possible to describe the item they chose. When you say "Go!", the students should pick up their pencils and begin writing. Give them three minutes to complete this challenge. After the allotted time, collect all the papers. Check to be sure that all the words are adjectives and that they can be applied to the given item. For this particular event, spelling does not count. The students who have the greatest numbers of adjectives are the winners.

# What's in a Name?

Words turn into names in this fun activity.

**Materials:**

Pencils and paper

**Activity:**

1. Discuss the following information with your class:
   Parents always choose the first names for their children. People have had last names for about 900 years. When people began to live together in villages, several people often had the same first name. This caused confusion. So, if there were two Williams in a village, people might call one "William, who is the carpenter," and the other "William, who is Ander's son." After a while the names were shortened to William Carpenter and William Anderson. Some last names came from people's jobs, such as Weaver, Miller, and Wheeler. Other names came from places people lived, such as Woods, Stone, or Brooks. When people have a special skill or physical characteristic they are sometimes given a name to fit that identifying feature. Someone called Red probably has that color hair; Chance might like to do a lot of wild things; and Tex might always wear a cowboy hat.

2. Tell the students that in this activity they will use common words and single letters to create names of people that match the jobs they hold. Here are a few hints to get them started:

   - Think of common nouns that can also be used as names.
   - Use letter names to help create a name, placing the letter as though it were an initial.
   - Think of names that sound like action words.

   **Some examples are:**
   | | |
   |---|---|
   | florist: | Rose Petal |
   | music teacher: | Carrie A. Tune |
   | glass maker: | Crystal Clear |
   | book reviewer: | Paige Turner |
   | weatherperson: | Sonny N. Warm |

3. Students should attempt to come up with at least 10 names and their corresponding professions.

# Vocabulary Baseball

In this activity, students round the bases by continuing to come up with new words and phrases.

## Materials:

Representation of a baseball diamond; game tokens (optional); 34 small squares of cardboard; a box, bag, or basket; colored markers

## Preparation:

1. For this game you will need to create a baseball diamond. This may be done by outlining bases with masking tape on the floor of your classroom. Or you could draw the diamond on a large poster or the chalkboard, or make an overhead transparency showing all the bases. If the children are not going to be moving around the bases themselves, you will need tokens of some type to indicate their movement.

2. Write one letter of the alphabet on each of the cardboard squares to create a set of letter tiles. On the remaining eight squares, print the word "OUT." Put all the squares in a box or basket.

## Activity:

1. Divide the class into two teams. For easy reference they will be referred to here as the Red and Blue teams.

2. Player number one from the Red team comes up to bat. A player from the Blue team acts as the pitcher and pulls out a letter tile from the box. He or she calls out the letter written on the tile.

3. The player at bat must come up with one, two, or three words that begin with that letter. If more than one word is given the words must form an understandable phrase, and each word must start with the "pitched" letter.

> **Example:** the letter B
> Acceptable answer: bad, bald bear
> Unacceptable answer: bat, beagle, brown

How to Teach Vocabulary Without Going Crazy • ©1999 Monday Morning Books

4. If a player comes up with one word, he hits a "single"; two words count as a "double"; and three words score a "triple." Batters move around the bases following the correct rules of baseball. Base runners advance one base per base hit. In other words, if the first person hits a single and the second player scores a double, the team has runners on second and third.

5. If the player at bat is unable to come up with any word beginning with the pitched letter, that player is "out."

6. If the Blue team draws a square with the word "OUT" written on it, then the player from the Red team is out until the next time he or she comes up in the batting order.

7. Three outs and the side is retired. When the Red team is retired, the Blue team has its turn at bat and the Red team does the pitching.

8. Play continues in this manner for up to nine innings.

**Notes:**

1. Once a letter is "pitched" it should be set aside. Return letter tiles to the box only after each full inning has been completed.

2. A player may not repeat a phrase that has already been used to score a base hit. A single must always result from a new word. A double may include one previously used word and one new word. A triple must incorporate at least two new words.

3. You may wish to have several students act as umpires. Umpires should write down the words used by the players and declare a "foul ball" if a player reuses a word in an illegal manner. If a foul ball is declared, the player is given one more chance to score a hit.

# Descriptive Designs

Pictures and words tell the story.

**Materials:**

Drawing paper; crayons, markers, or colored pencils; a thesaurus for each student

**Activity:**

1. Tell the students that they are going to create pictures enhanced by words.

2. Have students think about an animal or object for which they can think of 10 to 15 adjectives or descriptive phrases. Help students to use the thesaurus if they have trouble thinking of words.

3. Give each student a sheet of drawing paper on which to make an outline drawing of the subject that was chosen. Students should keep their drawings fairly simple.

4. Around the edge of the outline have the students write all the words that they think of to describe their animal or object.

5. Once the words have been written, ask the children to add some details to their pictures' background.

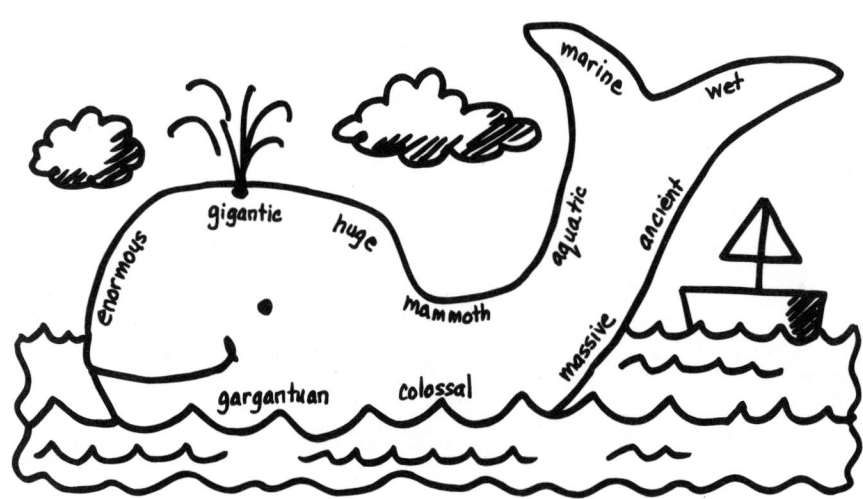

# Paint a Word Picture

Naming paint colors helps students focus on the nuance of words.

**Materials:**
Paint chip samples, pencils and paper

**Preparation:**
Obtain paint chip color samples from any home improvement store. Remove most of the names of the samples but keep a few intact to share as examples.

**Activity:**
1. Read several of the paint sample names to the class. Discuss how many of the names are lyrical and appealing. Read several other color names to the children without showing the samples. Ask the students to picture in their minds the color they think of when they hear those words. Point out that the name Island Breeze brings to mind a very different color than Sleek Steel.

2. Let each student choose five colors and come up with a name for each sample.

3. After students have given all their paint chips a name, have them prepare and give a brief oral presentation in which they attempt to sell one of their new colors. The presentation should include some justification for their name choice.

# A Thesaurus Is Not a Dinosaur

If students have never used a thesaurus, explain that it is a book that contains lists of synonyms, or words that have similar meanings. To use a dictionary you must know a word to look up its meaning. To use a thesaurus you begin with a concept or idea and find a word that best expresses it.

Tell the students that each entry in a thesaurus consists of:

- the entry word
- the part of speech
- synonyms
- a cross-reference to other similar words

Sometimes a thesaurus entry also includes brief definitions and a list of antonyms, or words that have the opposite meaning.

A thesaurus generally has two sections. Part one is an alphabetical listing, naming words and synonyms. Part two is a numbered section in which you find many synonyms and associated words. With this type of thesaurus, students should first look up the word or concept in the alphabetical section. There they will be given a number to turn to in the numerical listing.

A paperback thesaurus may have a simpler format. It may contain only alphabetical listings of words followed by their synonyms. These entries generally contain a "see also" note that sends the reader to another similar set of words. Be sure you are familiar with which type of thesaurus your students are using.

By middle school, most students are used to using a dictionary. However, many students are unfamiliar with the use of a thesaurus. You will need to take some time to let the students practice looking up words and finding the cross-references indicated. The following two activities will help students become more confident in their use of the thesaurus.

# Thesaurus Treasure Hunt

This activity helps familiarize students with the thesaurus.

**Materials:**

Paper and pencils, a thesaurus for each student, index cards, markers

**Preparation:**

Create about 40 activity cards. Number index cards from 1 through 40 and write a task on each that you want students to complete using a thesaurus. Here are some examples to get you started.

- List five synonyms for <u>good</u>.
- Find at least two synonyms for the underlined word (remember to stay close to the original meaning): Jacob will <u>explain</u> the mystery later.
- Fill in the blank with a synonym for <u>like</u>: Many people _____ movies.
- List two antonyms for <u>big</u>.
- Rewrite this sentence using a synonym for each underlined word: Marshall <u>saw</u> a <u>small</u> lizard <u>run</u> across the <u>road</u>.
- List four other words you could use to describe something <u>blue</u>.
- Find six words that could be used instead of <u>harbor</u>.

**Activity:**

1. Give one activity card to each student. Place the remaining cards on a table or in a box. Have the students write the number of their card on their paper. Then have them use a thesaurus to complete the task written on the card.

2. When the students have completed the task, they should trade in their card for a new one. Following the same procedure, they should write down the number of the new card and complete the task. Students should continue working in this manner until they have completed at least 10 tasks or worked for a specified amount of time.

# Presto Change-O

Synonyms are a great way to change and enliven student writing.

**Materials:**
Paper and pencils, a thesaurus for each student, a writing selection, staplers

**Preparation:**
Each student will need a copy of a writing selection that is no more than two paragraphs long. The selection may be cut from a newspaper or magazine, or be an excerpt from a basal reader or novel. It is recommended that all students use the same selection. If you need to make adjustments to suit the abilities of your class, try using one easier and one harder selection.

**Activity:**
1. Read over the writing selection with the class. Tell the students to look for words in the writing sample that they feel have several synonyms.

2. Have the students underline 10–15 words that they believe they can find in the thesaurus.

3. Ask the class to rewrite the selection by replacing the words they have underlined with synonyms. Remind students that the replacement words must be close enough in definition to the originals that they do not greatly alter the context of the paragraphs. As they rewrite the selection, students should underline the synonyms they use.

4. Have students staple their own work and the original work together before handing in the assignment.

# Tom Swifties

Tom Swift was a young, adventurous hero created by the author Edward Stratemeyer. During the early part of the 20th century, Tom Swift adventure stories were very popular with children. In the stories, Tom and his friends never just said something. Instead, they always said it quickly, happily, or doubtfully. Today, "Tom Swifties" are adverb quotations that result in a pun.

**Materials:**
Paper and pencils, dictionary for each student, thesaurus for each student

**Activity:**
1. Share the above information with the students.

2. Brainstorm a list of adverbs with the class. Remind students that adverbs tell how an action is done. Also remind students that many adverbs end with the -ly suffix. This hint will help them add words to the list.

3. Once the list has been made, share several examples of Tom Swifties. Have students note that what Tom says and how he says it are related in some way, creating a joke or pun.

> **Examples:**
> "This shirt is wrinkled," said Tom ironically.
> "This knife is very sharp," said Tom cuttingly.
> "I love pancakes," said Tom flippantly.
> "My favorite pie is lemon meringue," said Tom tartly.

4. Have the students study the above examples. Ask them to point out the relationship between what was said and how it was said. Refer to the list of adverbs. Develop several Tom Swifties as a class.

5. Tell students that they are to write some Tom Swiftie puns on their own. They may refer to the brainstorming list or use a thesaurus or dictionary if they need help finding more adverbs. Have the students write at least five Tom Swifties each. If time allows, let students share some of their puns with the entire class.

# Specialties

Discovering words that pertain to special fields or activities is an excellent way to increase vocabulary.

**Materials:**

Paper and pencils, index cards

**Activity:**

1. Explain to the class that various sports, hobbies, and professions have specialized vocabularies all their own. Have students share their knowledge of any words that are specific to a particular activity. For example, here are some words that are used in the sport of rock climbing:

> beta–advice
> dyno–upward lunge
> talis–boulders at the base of a cliff
> talis food–what you are if you fall

2. Give the students the following assignment:

> a. Choose a sport, activity, craft, hobby, or profession. It may be one you are familiar with or one you would like to learn more about.
> b. Find at least 10 words that are specific to your chosen activity. Write down each word and its definition.
> c. You may use books or magazines or interview friends and relatives.

3. Once the lists of words have been compiled, divide the class into groups. You may want to have a "sports" group, a "craft" group, etc. Have students share their lists in the group. Then pass out an index card to each student. The students should write their words and definitions on the index card. If two or more students chose an identical or similar activity, have them combine and organize their words. Be sure that the children title each list. Keep the cards in a file at a reading or writing center.

# Groovy!

Nothing makes time-period pieces come more alive than the use of colorful slang.

**Materials:**

Paper and pencils, markers, large pieces of newsprint

**Activity:**

1. Tell students that slang is an intrinsic part of our culture. Sometimes slang words become so popular that they are accepted as everyday language and added to the dictionary. "Groovy" is an example of just such a word. However, slang words are usually here today and gone tomorrow.

Slang terms can be a useful tool in writing, helping to lend authenticity to a period piece. For example, if students are writing about the '50s, then "nifty" and "keen" can add color. A story about a '70s hippie will be more believable if the hippie mumbles "I need some bread for groovy threads" rather than "I am in need of money to purchase some nice clothes." Share some slang with the class from your favorite era.

2. Have students compile a list of their favorite, school-appropriate slang. Set strict limits here and make yourself very clear on what terms will be accepted for use in your classroom.

3. Assign students the homework of interviewing parents or grandparents about popular slang they recall. Students should write down the words or phrases and their meanings. In class, compile a list of words that the students have discovered. Write these on a piece of newsprint.

4. Create a class "What's Hot, What's Not" list of words. Place these two headings in column fashion on a piece of newsprint. Under "What's Hot," have students list slang words that are used now. The "What's Not" column is for last year's discards.

5. Have students take some of the slang that has been collected by the class and incorporate it into a writing assignment. You may want to suggest a time travel theme for their stories.

Groovy

Cool

Bad

Slick

Boss

Sweet

# Analogies

Making and using analogies help stretch the imagination.

**Materials:**

Paper and pencils, vocabulary list

**Activity:**

1. Explain to the class that analogies are a form of comparison. There are four types of analogies.

> word : synonym
> word : antonym
> object : activity
> activity : object

2. Go over the language of analogies with students. When something is written like this—"happy : glad : : unhappy : sad"— it is read "happy is to glad as unhappy is to sad." This is an example of a word : synonym comparison. The first two words in the analogy mean the same thing and the last two words also have a similar meaning.

A synonym : antonym analogy example is **"night : day : : dark : light."** In this analogy the first two words are opposite and the last two words are also antonyms of each other.

An object : activity example is **"bat : baseball : : racket : tennis."** With this type of analogy, the first word is an item that is needed in order to participate in the second word of the comparison.

An activity : object example is **"sculpting : clay : : sewing : material."** This analogy first presents the action, then something used when involved in that particular activity.

3. Have students create analogies using their list of vocabulary words as a starting point. Tell students that they should try to include all four types of analogies in their assignment.

# Alpha Hunt

One letter—11 new words.

**Materials:**

Paper and pencils, dictionaries, colored paper, marker, scissors

**Preparation:**

Cut the colored paper into small squares. Make enough squares so that you have about five more than the number of students in your class. On each square write a consonant or a vowel. It is best to use the more common consonants, although you can use the more uncommon ones at a later time.

**Activity:**

1. Have the students number their papers from 2 to 12, numbering every other line.

2. Spread the letter squares face down on a table. Let each student come up and pick a square. This is the letter that he or she will use for the Alpha Hunt.

3. Explain to the students that they are going to try to find words that begin with the letter they have picked. The first word should be two letters long. They are to write the word on the line with the corresponding number. The word should be followed by its definition. The next word they write must be three letters long, and so on, up to 12 letters. The students should use their dictionaries to help them with this assignment.

> **Example:**
> 2 **so** therefore
> 3 **sic** to command a dog to attack
> 4 **scud** to move quickly or be driven by the wind
> 5 **shill** a partner in a carnival game
> 6 **schism** a split between parties due to a difference in opinion
> 7 **skeptic** a person who is hard to convince
> 8 **skirmish** a brief, unimportant conflict
> 9 **sociology** the science of social relations
> 10 **slenderize** to make or become slender
> 11 **squalidness** state of being rundown and unclean
> 12 **statistician** a person who studies statistics

4. Let the class know that for some letters there may be no two-letter word. In this case the student should just write "none" on the line next to the number two. Also tell students that the more unique each word is, the better. Give extra credit to students who are able to extend their list to 13 or more letters.

5. You may want to have students complete this exercise for several different letters. Once their lists have been compiled, have the children add at least five of the new words to their journals.

6. Here are some ways to use the lists that the students gathered:

- Have a spelling contest using the longer words.
- Make a class word file by having the students transfer the lists to index cards.
    Have students write the lists in alphabetical order on each of the cards, then file the cards in alphabetical order. Students may use the file as a resource for creative writing.
- Have students write a paragraph using at least five of the words they discovered.
- Let students choose one of the longer words. Then assign them the task of creating as many words as possible by just using the letters contained in the chosen word.
- Have students write each word in a sentence.
- Award extra credit to anyone who is able to find one of his or her words in a newspaper or magazine article.

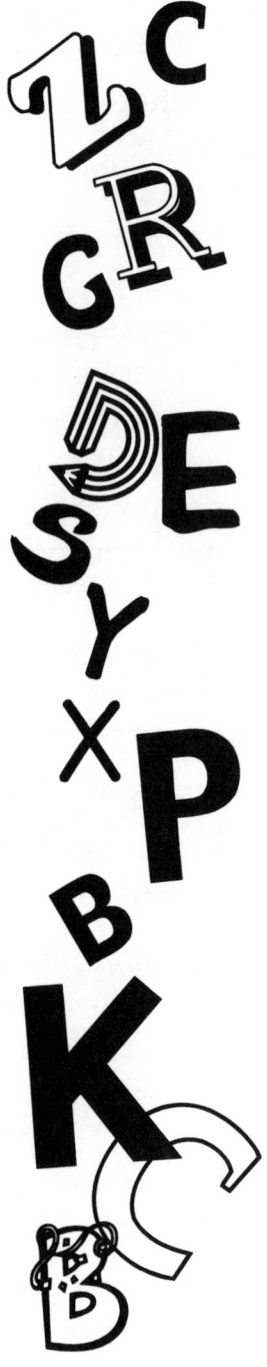

# Language Guardians

Students are given the assignment of deciding on 25 of the most important words.

**Materials:**

Paper and pencils, vocabulary journals

**Activity:**

1. Ask students to imagine that the class has been named as a "language guardian" for a new baby. The students' job is to help the baby learn to speak. The problem is that they may teach the baby only 25 words.

2. Brainstorm awhile with the class about the types of words that might be the most important. Have the students concentrate on ways they communicate their needs and wants. Ask them to consider which words are vital and which words can be understood without speaking them. For example, you could point to parts of the body without knowing the names for them. However, you would want to know the word hurt or pain in order to communicate a need for medical help.

3. Challenge each student to come up with the 25 words that he or she feels are the most important for the baby to know. This is a tough enterprise, so allow plenty of time for its completion. Students should write a brief statement as to why they feel each particular word they chose is vital.

**Examples:**

love—an emotion all humans crave
hungry—a word used to express a specific need
Mom—the most important person in my life
Dad—another very important person
Grandpa—often a source for toys and treats
help—very useful for gaining assistance

*food*
*toy*
*milk*
*laugh*
*sleepy*
*diaper*
*brother*
*Grandma*

*bottle*
*blanket*
*hug*
*rattle*
*spoon*

*pudding*
*baby*
*pillow*
*book*
*pamper*

4. Be sure to allow for some interaction time after the students complete their lists. Small groups work well for discussions. Have students compare lists to determine which words appear on everyone's list or on a majority of lists. After hearing the opinions of others in their group, give students a chance to revise their own choices before handing in the assignment.

# Wondrous Wallpaper

Wallpaper samples can help students with descriptive writing.

**Materials:**

Wallpaper samples, paper and pencil, drawing paper (optional)

**Preparation:**

Outdated wallpaper sample books are generally available for little or no cost from home improvement stores. Browse through the books and cut out squares for each student to have one.

**Procedure:**

1. Pass out a wallpaper sample to each student. Tell the class that they are to imagine a setting where this wallpaper might be found.

2. Give the following assignment to the students.

> • Describe the room where this wallpaper is found.
> • Describe the kind of house or building where the room is located.
> • Give a description of the setting or location of the house.
> • Develop at least two characters to inhabit the house.
> • List three characteristics for each character.
> • Write a short story that takes place in the setting you described and involves the characters that you created.

3. Optional: Have students draw a picture of the room they have described. Let students cut up the wallpaper sample and glue some of this to one or more of the walls in the room. Attach the stories to the drawings.

# Travel Brochures

Students create their own travel pamphlets using words and pictures that specifically relate to their topic.

**Materials:**
Paper and pencils, drawing paper, markers or colored pencils, travel brochures

**Preparation:**
Call a wide variety of the 800 numbers in travel magazines. Travel personnel will be happy to send you brochures on resorts, theme parks, restaurants, shopping malls, and the like. Try to obtain one brochure for each student; however, the activity may be done by partners.

**Activity:**
1. Pass out the brochures to the class. Give students time to read them over. Spend some time discussing the type of words used in the text. Are the words trying to create a specific mood? Romantic restaurants will use phrases such as *candlelight setting*, *exquisite dining*, and *fine wines*. A family resort will try to be convincing with *something for everyone*, *exciting water slides*, and *fun, fun, fun*. Discuss the types of pictures that are used to promote the various concepts.

2. Have each student make a list of descriptive phrases used in his or her brochure. Let the children determine the type of mood the pamphlet is trying to convey.

3. Tell the class that they are going to design their own travel brochures. Have students first decide on the type of place they will be promoting. Be flexible in allowing students to choose fantasy places, such as moon resorts, underwater restaurants, etc. A brochure might also be about a spot the student has actually visited.

4. Students should first create a rough draft that includes phrases and picture sketches that they will use in their brochure. When this is complete, pass out the drawing paper and have the children create their travel pamphlets.

5. Allow time for each student to make a brief oral presentation about his or her special brochure.

# Concrete Poetry

Vocabulary words take shape in this poetry/picture exercise.

**Materials:**

Unlined paper; pencils, pens, or colored pencils; samples of concrete poetry

**Activity:**

1. Introduce concrete poetry to the class—poetry that is created when words are written in the shape of the subject. Show several examples. For this particular exercise, nouns will be used, although you may also want to allow some adjectives to be included.

2. Tell students to choose a simple subject for their poem. It should be an object that contains a number of different parts, allowing a number of nouns to describe it. For example, a ball would not be a very suitable subject since there are few nouns that could be used to describe it. A car has many more parts and therefore would work well for this project.

3. After each student has chosen a subject, have the children write a list of as many related nouns as they can think of to use in their poem.

> **Example:** car
> hood, headlight, bumper, door, windshield, trunk, tire, hubcap, roof, chassis, window

4. Students now choose words from their list to use in the design of their poem. The words should be written in such a manner that the image of the subject is apparent.

door
windshield
trunk
headlight
roof
window
hubcap
trunk
chassis
tire
headlight
hood

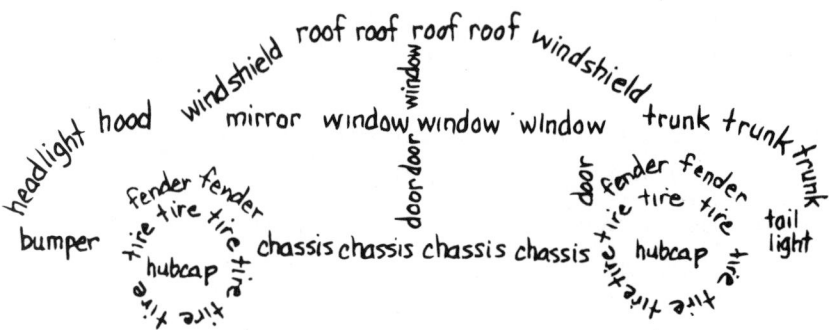

# Alpha Lists

Alphabet-based exercises provide a wide range of activities that encourage children to seek out and use new words. Try one or more of the following projects.

**Materials:**
Drawing paper and colored construction paper; markers, crayons, or colored pencils; writing paper and pencils; stapler or yarn and needle; scissors; dictionaries; vocabulary journals; ABC books

**Activity:**
1. Have the students list the letters of the alphabet down the left side of their paper. Announce a topic, such as animals, sports, food, or movies. Ask the students to write one word for each letter of the alphabet that pertains to that specific subject.

2. Give your class this challenge: Write the letters of the alphabet down one side of your paper. Try to come up with one word for each letter that relates to the topic but that you feel no one else will discover. Use the dictionary for help. Be sure to learn the correct pronunciation and definition of each new word.

After the lists are complete, ask one student to read his or her words. If any one else has listed a word that was read, both students cross out that word. As more students read from their lists, remind them not to read any of the words that have been crossed out. Continue until everyone has shared a list. Give a prize to the student with the most unique words. Have students add some of these words to their journals.

3. Tell the class that they are going to design Alpha List posters. Give each student a piece of drawing paper. Tell the students to write the letters of the alphabet down the left edge of the paper. Encourage the students to make the letters in a colorful and attractive manner.

Using dictionaries and journals, students should come up with five words for each letter. These should be written next to the corresponding letter. When all the posters are complete, staple or stitch them together to form a Big Book. Place the book in an area where students may use it as a free reading option.

4. Borrow a variety of ABC picture books from the library. Tell the class that although the books are designed for very young children, they are going to develop their own books using a similar format. Students should first choose a subject that interests them, that they know a lot about, or that they wish to learn more about. Encourage each child to choose a broad subject. For example, it would be difficult to make an ABC book on dolphins, but quite appropriate to make one on marine animals. Once the students have chosen their subject, they need to come up with one word for every letter of the alphabet that pertains to their chosen topic. Some of the letters will be more difficult, so discuss ways to incorporate them into the book. For example zooming dolphins could work with Z, quiet squid with Q. Try to allow time for a session or two in the library, since most students will need to do some research on their subjects.

Once all the words have been chosen, have the students begin to create their books. Each page should contain a letter of the alphabet along with its matching word or phrase and an illustration. Have the children use a sheet of colored construction paper to form the front and back covers of their book. Let the students illustrate their covers.

Because the children will want to see the books their classmates have created, be sure to give them time to share the finished books. You might also want to arrange a get-together with a class of younger children and have your students read their books to them.

> **Possible ABC picture book topics:**
>
> | | | | |
> |---|---|---|---|
> | seasons | reptiles | fish | Olympic sports |
> | birds | astronomy | cars | medieval times |
> | movies | pets | fashion | rock stars |
> | food | plants | countries | theme parks |
> | dinosaurs | weather | art | science fiction |
> | architecture | jobs | music | TV shows |

# TOPIC-SPECIFIC ACTIVITIES

This section of the book contains a variety of vocabulary lists. The words in these lists relate to a topic or a theme. Since vocabulary is not limited to singular words, several lists introduce proverbs, figurative language, acronyms, and initialisms. The vocabulary is designed to focus on language arts subjects as well as cross over into other curriculum areas.

Most of the lists are comprised of 20 words—but there is nothing sacred about the number 20. Depending on the ages and abilities of your students, you will want to adapt the lists to fit your needs. If you are working with younger children, the number of words should be reduced. At times you may wish to use only five words from a list; at other times you may want to expand a list to more than 20.

Along with each list there are three or more activities that correlate directly to the words in the list. These activities do not seek to have the students memorize the vocabulary and definitions. Rather, they allow students to use the new words and provide opportunities for the children to relate the vocabulary to their own experiences. Pick and choose the lessons you feel will be beneficial to your students. Do look over all the options listed; in some cases one activity builds upon a previous one.

In order to provide lessons and projects for fourth through eighth grades, a wide range of skill levels is included. Once again, you will need to customize the lessons to the age and abilities of your class. Keep in mind that if your expectations are high, most students tend to rise to the challenge.

If you have opted to use the journal format in your classroom, the lists provide an array of words that may be added to them. For example, if you are working to help students broaden their use of adjectives, then you will want students to add several complete lists of adjectives to their journals. Or you may want to focus on only a few new words and have students add only these to their journals. Just be sure that the students use their journals in their everyday writing. Don't let the journals sit in a corner gathering dust until the next time you have the children add a few new words. Encourage students to add more words than the ones you require.

As you work with the activities and lists, you may find they act as springboards to wonderful ideas of your own. Students also may find ways to improve and adapt the activities, so try to remain flexible in your assessment of their success. Above all, make the experience of vocabulary building an enjoyable one!

# JOBS

| | | | |
|---|---|---|---|
| accountant | author | banker | carpenter |
| chef | chemist | electrician | executive |
| firefighter | judge | lawyer | machinist |
| manager | pharmacist | plumber | police officer |
| programmer | scientist | secretary | waitress |

1. Discuss with students the type of work each job in the list represents. Have students work in small groups to brainstorm as many jobs or careers as they can.

2. Have the children create a large collage of pictures cut from magazines that represent the various jobs.

3. Play the Mystery Person Game. Each student chooses a particular job and writes 5 to 10 clues that tell about the job without actually naming it. Each student then comes forward and begins to read the clues. The class tries to guess the person who is being described. Students will want to come up with some tough clues to try to stump the class. Giving very general information in the clues will also make the class work harder to solve the mystery. Tell students that their early clues should give general information and then progress to more specific details.

> **Example clues:**
> 1. may work indoors or outdoors
> 2. must understand how to measure
> 3. uses tools
> 4. must be able to read blueprints
> 5. has a job in the construction business
> 6. needs to understand electricity
>
> Answer: electrician

4. Have a mini-career fair. Assign students to interview relatives or friends about their jobs. Each student should create a poster about one particular job. The poster should include information as well as illustrations that pertain to the job. Set aside a time for students to present the information they have compiled.

5. Invite speakers to come to the classroom to share information about their jobs.

# FIRST AID

| | | | |
|---|---|---|---|
| abrasion | antiseptic | bandage | bleeding |
| breathing | bruise | burn | calm |
| choking | cleanse | concussion | fracture |
| poison | pressure | shock | sling |
| splint | sprain | victim | wound |

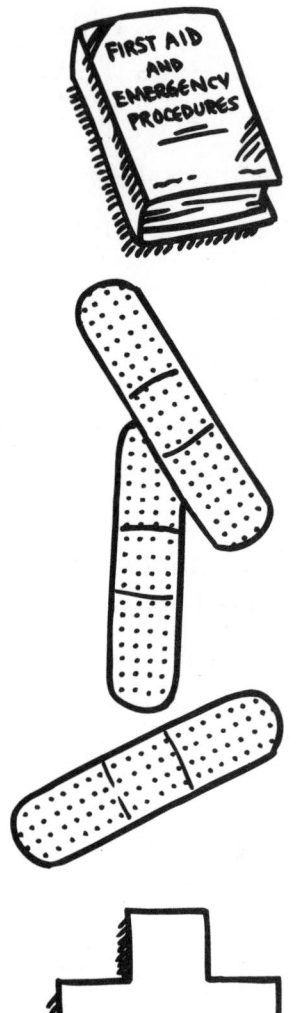

1. Have a speaker come to your class and demonstrate first-aid techniques. Possible resources: Red Cross worker, Scout leader, Boy or Girl Scout who is a member of your class, park ranger, nurse.

2. Help students to make small, inexpensive pocket first-aid kits for themselves. These are handy to take on bike rides, picnics, or rollerblading.

Ahead of time, take a large cake of soap and cut it into small chunks about the size of centimeter cubes. Be sure to have enough cubes so that every child can have one in the kit. For each kit you will also need an antiseptic wipe and two or three adhesive bandages, plus a small plastic bag with a zipper closing to store everything in. (Your parent-teacher organization may be willing to provide funding for this project; or a local pharmacy or clinic might be willing to donate the items.) Provide index cards for each student. Have the students write on the cards some first aid tips they feel are important and add the cards to their kits.

3. Check out books from the library that give instructions on first aid. Give your class an opportunity to look at these books. Using the first-aid manuals as a resource, have students work in groups to create posters about first aid. Topics could include instructions for emergencies or safety messages. Display the posters around the school as a public service project.

How to Teach Vocabulary Without Going Crazy • ©1999 Monday Morning Books

# THE BIG PICTURE

| broad | bulky | colossal | enormous |
|---|---|---|---|
| expansive | extensive | gigantic | grandiose |
| huge | immense | large | mammoth |
| massive | monumental | oversized | spacious |
| stout | towering | tremendous | vast |

1. Have students create collages from magazine pictures of things that could be described by the adjectives on this list (skyscrapers, jets, elephants, ships, stadiums, etc.).

2. Let the students use chalk to write the vocabulary words on the playground or sidewalk. Be sure that the words are written using "gigantic" letters.

3. Start collecting a list of advertisements that use any of the adjectives. Have students bring in any that are in printed form. If the children hear the adjectives used on the radio or television, have them write down the product being described and the phrase used to add to the collection.

4. Give students this story starter:

> I woke up this morning and hit my head on the ceiling. I couldn't even stand up straight. I looked in the mirror to discover I was enormous. What happens next?

5. View the movie <u>Honey, I Shrunk the Kids!</u> or <u>The Incredible Shrinking Woman.</u> If you are short on time, just view several segments. As the students watch the movie, have them write a descriptive phrase that relates to each of several scenes they view. Each phrase should include a different vocabulary word.

> **Examples:**
> a colossal bowl
> a mammoth telephone
> a swarm of gigantic bees
> Legos in a towering stack

# INSTEAD OF SAID

| announced | asked | assured | commented |
|-----------|-------|---------|-----------|
| complained | explained | groaned | implored |
| informed | insisted | moaned | mumbled |
| questioned | reminded | replied | screamed |
| squealed | stated | whispered | yelled |

1. Provide the class with a wide selection of comic strips from the newspaper. Have students look at what is being said in the individual panels. Tell students to choose a vocabulary word and write it under an appropriate panel, better describing how the character is delivering the dialogue.

> **Examples:**
> Garfield often has "moaned" his lines.
> Sarge has definitely "yelled" at Beetle Bailey.

Have students try to find at least one panel that illustrates each of the words on the list.

2. Play Charades with the class to show how facial expressions and body language help convey a word's meaning. Write each vocabulary word on a separate slip of paper. Have each student come forward in turn, pick a word, and try to act it out without using any sound.

3. Assign students a short story to write. Tell them it must include at least ten pieces of dialogue. The students may use any of the vocabulary words on the list, but "said" may <u>not</u> be used anywhere in the story.

4. Have the class write "Tom Swifties" (see p. 63 for details), replacing the word "said" with one of the vocabulary words.

> **Examples:**
> "This pillow is very comfortable," Tom whispered softly.
> "Go, team, go!", Tom screamed winningly.
> "I go to church every Sunday," Tom announced faithfully.

How to Teach Vocabulary Without Going Crazy • ©1999 Monday Morning Books

# ON THE ROAD

| | | | |
|---|---|---|---|
| avenue | boulevard | bypass | curb |
| drive | exit | highway | interchange |
| interstate | lane | median | overpass |
| ramp | road | route | shoulder |
| street | tollbooth | tollway | underpass |

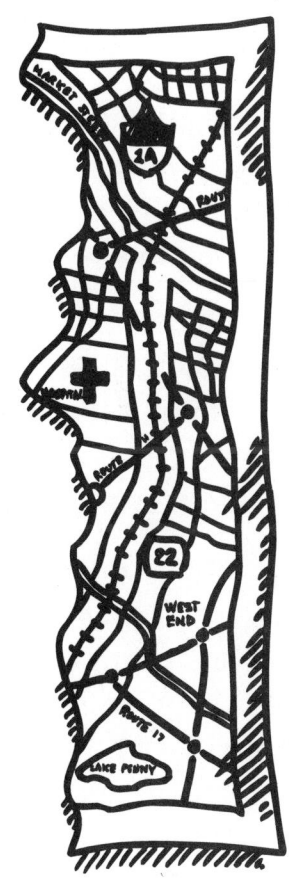

1. Have students tell the name of the street in their home address. Create a list of the names. Be sure to point out to students when the vocabulary word requires a capital. For example, in the phrase "walking down a road," "road" is a common noun and doesn't require a capital. In "walking down River Road," "Road" is a proper noun and does require a capital.

2. Obtain maps of your city and state. Have students identify as many of the vocabulary words on the map as possible.

3. Invite someone from the city engineer's or city manager's office to come in and speak to your class about how streets are named and maintained in your community.

4. Have students create their own maps of an imaginary community. Be sure that they include at least 10 of the vocabulary words on their maps. Allow time for each student to give an oral presentation about his or her community. The students should tell why they chose the particular names they did for the roadways on their maps.

5. Have the students, individually, in groups, or as a class, plan an imaginary cross-country trip. Have them begin in your community and "travel" to a destination that requires them to pass through at least five states. Tell the children to use a road atlas to determine the best route and to include some detours along the way for sightseeing. Have students make a complete list of routes that must be followed and the direction in which they will be headed on each route. Be sure that students use the correct names of highways and roadways. Include a writing assignment that lets students describe their journey.

# WAY BEYOND GOOD

| | | | |
|---|---|---|---|
| decent | delectable | delightful | elite |
| enjoyable | excellent | fascinating | grand |
| magnificent | matchless | optimum | prime |
| quintessential | satisfying | sensational | superb |
| superior | tremendous | virtuous | wonderful |

1. Have students design a menu for a fabulous restaurant. If possible, bring in some examples from restaurants or caterers that include descriptions of the food available. Suggested requirements for the menu: a name for the restaurant, at least 10 descriptions of different food items, illustrations, and prices. Menus may be created on large pieces of drawing paper.

2. Discuss with students the way commentators describe a championship sporting event. Have students give a performance that mimics this style. Be sure that their descriptions include the type of event and some of the star athletes present. Students should be sure to include as many vocabulary words as possible.

3. Tell students to pretend they are a movie or book critic and to write a positive review about a movie or book they enjoyed. Remind them to use vocabulary words but take time to note that describing something as "delightful, sensational, matchless, and magnificent" is overkill. Students don't need to use every vocabulary word, just greater variety than always using "good."

4. Give students a writing assignment with the story prompt:

The best day of my life. . . .

How to Teach Vocabulary Without Going Crazy • ©1999 Monday Morning Books

# MEDIEVAL TIMES

| | | | |
|---|---|---|---|
| apprentice | armor | castle | chivalry |
| court | decree | dragon | drawbridge |
| jester | joust | kingdom | knight |
| labyrinth | manor | moat | page |
| peasant | steed | sword | wizard |

1. Read aloud to the class <u>Max and Me and the Time Machine</u> by Gery Greer and Bob Ruddick. It's a quick read and fun for this topic.

2. Ask students to design a set for a play that takes place in medieval times. Tell them their designs should include as many items from the vocabulary list as possible. Provide drawing paper and markers, crayons, or colored pencils to create this project. Encourage students to add some three-dimensional touches to the designs by providing yarn, material, foil, etc.

3. Have students write a story that begins with this prompt:

> When I was walking through the park I crossed a bridge. Gradually I found myself getting deeper and deeper into a forest. Through the trees I could see a glittering castle.

4. As a class watch a movie that pertains to the topic, such as <u>A Connecticut Yankee in King Arthur's Court</u> or Disney's <u>Sword in the Stone.</u> While viewing the movie, students should write down sentences that describe scenes from the film. Each of these sentences should include a vocabulary word.

> **Examples:**
> Merlin and Wart swim as fish in the castle's moat.
> A page handed the knight his lance.

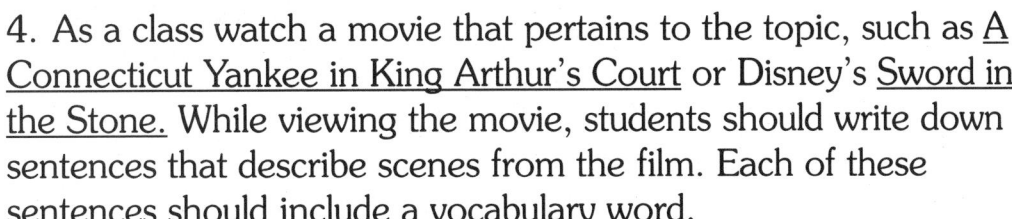

5. Ask students to create and present a project that relates to the topic. Some ideas: a diagram or model of a castle or one that depicts a joust or fair; a play about an apprentice; a painting of medieval times; a comic strip starring a wizard, knight, or peasant; a story about time traveling to medieval times.

# COMPOUNDS

| | | | |
|---|---|---|---|
| bookcase | boxcar | butterfly | cardboard |
| crosswalk | goldfish | moonlight | postcard |
| railroad | rainbow | raindrop | sandbox |
| scrapbook | shoestring | snowfall | snowman |
| stoplight | sunshine | treehouse | waterfall |

1. Have the students create puzzle pairs of the compound word vocabulary list. Provide squares of colored paper, markers, and scissors. Have students write one compound word on each rectangle, leaving a bit of space between the two parts of the compound. This will allow room for cutting the rectangle in half to create a puzzle. Let students reassemble their words and try to mix and match to form additional compounds.

2. Have the students use squares of drawing paper and markers, crayons, or colored pencils to create picture codes that can be placed together to create compound words. Provide squares of paper. On each square, have the students draw a representation of one of the smaller words found in the list of compounds. Let students know that they need only draw one "rain" card in order to form both raindrop and rainbow.

3. Host a compound word "Treasure Hunt." Provide a lot of written material in the form of books, magazines, and newspapers. Then divide the class into partners or groups of three. Instruct the children to search the materials and make a list of all the compound words they find. Have a prize for the group that comes up with the most words.

# ANIMAL ANATOMY

| | | | |
|---|---|---|---|
| beak | body | claws | ears |
| eyes | fangs | feathers | fin |
| fur | gills | head | hoof (hooves) |
| mane | nose | paws | scales |
| tail | talons | whiskers | wings |

1. Have the class write concrete poetry using an animal theme (see p. 72).

2. Ask each student to draw an animal or bring in a stuffed animal or an animal model. Have the students label each part of the animal's anatomy using words from the vocabulary list. Allow time for students to each give an oral presentation about the animal.

3. Have the children create Crazy Critters. Using a wide variety of art supplies (crayons, markers, fabric, fake feathers, colored pencils, paper scraps) have them mix and match animal parts to come up with imaginary creatures on large pieces of drawing paper. After the critters are complete, the children should list the animal's anatomy.

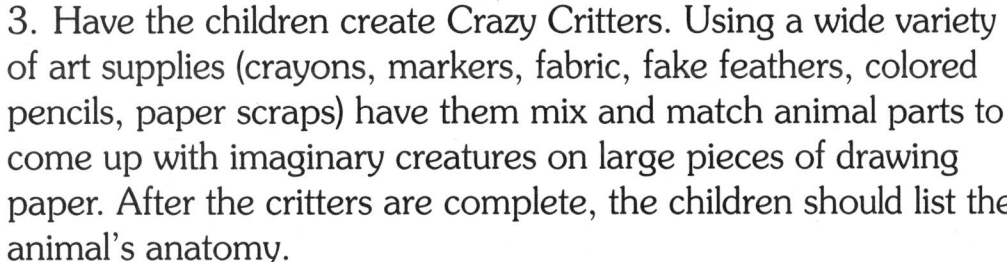

> **Example:**
> ear of a rabbit    alligator face
> mane of a lion    neck of a giraffe
> fish fin    horse's body and hoof
> wing of an eagle    rhinoceros leg
> tail of a panther

# FRUITS

| | | | |
|---|---|---|---|
| apple | apricot | banana | blueberries |
| cantaloupe | cherry | grapefruit | grapes |
| lemon | lime | mango | nectarine |
| orange | papaya | peach | pear |
| pineapple | plum | strawberries | watermelon |

1. Bring in some grocery advertisements from the newspapers. Have students cut out and label the various types of fruit. Create a class collage by having the children glue the pictures to a large piece of newsprint.

2. Bring in a few samples of recipe cards to show as examples. Point out to students the various standard parts of a recipe: name of dish, ingredients and amounts, procedure, baking or cooking instructions, number served, etc.

Have students follow the standard recipe format and create a fruit dish using as many of the vocabulary words as possible. When the rough drafts of the recipes have been edited, have the students rewrite final copies on index cards to begin a "Recipe File." This file can be placed in the reading center for some free time reading enjoyment.

3. Have a fruit-tasting party. Ask each student to bring in one type of fruit. Cut the fruit in very small pieces. Let students sample as many kinds of fruit as possible. Have students vote for their favorite fruit and make a graph of the results.

4. Have the class make flash cards of the vocabulary words. Students may draw pictures or cut them out from ads, magazines, or food labels. Tell the children to put the picture on one side of the card and its corresponding vocabulary word on the back of the card. Have them make one card for each word. Let students use the flash cards with a partner to quiz each other on the words.

# RAIN FOREST

| | | | |
|---|---|---|---|
| anteater | butterflies | cacao (chocolate) | canopy |
| capybara | ferns | frogs | katydid |
| lemur | macaw | mahogany | monkey |
| orchid | rainfall | salamander | tapir |
| toads | toucan | undergrowth | waterfall |

1. Have students choose ten of the plants or animals from the list. Then have them research their choices and write three facts about each. After the students have completed this activity, have them choose their favorite plant or animal. Group students who have the same favorites. Allow time for the groups to organize the facts that each student obtained. Have each group make a short oral presentation to the class about its chosen subject.

2. Ask the students to write letters to the editor of your local newspaper about why our rain forests should be saved. Before starting, hold a review of letter writing form. When the children write their letters, be sure they give sound reasons for their request. Encourage them to include information about ways that everyone can help (by not buying tropical wood products, by purchasing renewable crop items such as nuts and fruits from the area).

3. Involve the students in creating coloring pages for children in earlier grades. Show your class a coloring book or several coloring sheets to illustrate that when a coloring page is drawn, only the outlines are given and sometimes some background details. Point out that there are lots of different size spaces to be colored in. Let each student draw the outlines of a coloring page about the rain forest. They may use a pencil to make the drawing, then go over the lines with a black pen. At the bottom of the page, students should write an informational sentence or two that tells something about the picture they have drawn.

# OUTDOOR ADVENTURE

| backpack | bicycle | binoculars | camp |
| --- | --- | --- | --- |
| campfire | canoe | cave | climb |
| compass | desert | fishing | forest |
| hike | mountain | raft | rapids |
| stream | tent | trail | wildlife |

1. Using drawing paper and colored pencils, markers, or crayons, the students should design a map of a place that would be a good location for an outdoor adventure. Remind students to use as many vocabulary words as possible as they create and name the places on their maps.

2. Have students write stories about the maps they have designed. Or give students these titles as story starters:

> "The Ultimate Adventure," "An Extreme Experience," "A Time Never to Be Forgotten," "The Wilderness and Me."

3. Read selected passages from the story <u>Hatchet</u> by Gary Paulsen.

4. Play a variation of the Fishing Game. For this game you will need 40 fish shapes cut from colored paper. On 20 fish write one vocabulary word. On each of the other 20 fish write a definition of a vocabulary word. Bend a large paper clip so that it resembles a fish hook. Spread all the fish, writing side down, on the floor. Tape a line on the floor or use a meter stick to indicate where players should stand. The first player tosses the hook at the fish. The player "catches" whichever fish the hook lands on. If the hook doesn't land on a fish, it is the next player's turn. The player reads what is on the fish that was caught. If it is a definition, then the player calls on someone in the class to provide the vocabulary word. If the word is read, then someone must supply the definition. After the correct answer is given, the fish is removed from the game. If the answer is incorrect, the fish is put back into the game. Play continues until all the fish have been caught.

# ZOO

| | | | |
|---|---|---|---|
| alligator | bear | chimpanzee | elephant |
| flamingo | giraffe | gorilla | habitat |
| hyena | kangaroo | leopard | llama |
| peacock | rhinoceros | snake | tiger |
| turtle | wolf | zebra | zookeeper |

1. Have the children create a diorama or other three-dimensional model of a zoo. Be sure that they label each of the animals represented.

2. Tell students to each choose one animal. They are to research that animal and learn five facts about it. Once the information has been gathered, have the students present their facts in an oral presentation.

3. Have the class design "Zoo Cards." Use the large-size index cards to develop this project. Ask each student to draw a picture of an animal on the unlined side of the card. On the lined side, they should list facts about the animal, including length, weight, habitat, eating habits, name given to the babies of the species, and any other special facts. The students may choose other animals besides those on the vocabulary list. Give extra credit to students who write about a very unusual animal or who discover a unique fact about a certain creature. Keep all the cards in a file box or zipper-style plastic bag, and add them to the reading center if desired.

4. Just for fun, read <u>If I Ran the Zoo</u> by Dr. Seuss. Then have students write a story or poem about a zoo, including as many vocabulary words as possible.

# WEATHER

| | | | |
|---|---|---|---|
| barometer | blizzard | clouds | drizzle |
| drought | forecast | front | hail |
| highs | hurricane | lows | mild |
| pressure | rain | sleet | snow |
| storm | sunny | temperature | wind |

1. For at least a week, have the class collect daily weather reports from the newspapers. Discuss and define the terms found in the reports. Circle any vocabulary words that are written in the article.

2. Using the daily weather reports, keep a class graph of the high and low temperatures in your area. You may want to expand the venture and make other graphs for cities around the nation.

3. Use a map of the world. As a class, attach labels that indicate the type of weather being experienced in various locations.

4. Have students pretend to be weather forecasters for any city. Ask them to give an oral presentation on the long-range forecast for their chosen region. Weather reports from the Internet are very useful for this project. Information may also be gathered from newspapers or by watching a national weather forecast.

   *How to Teach Vocabulary Without Going Crazy* • ©1999 Monday Morning Books

# VEGETABLES

| | | | |
|---|---|---|---|
| **asparagus** | **beans** | **beets** | **broccoli** |
| **cabbage** | **carrots** | **cauliflower** | **celery** |
| **corn** | **leek** | **onion** | **peas** |
| **pepper** | **potato** | **radish** | **spinach** |
| **tomato** | **turnip** | **yam** | **zucchini** |

1. Discuss the various vegetables with the children. Let them share their likes and dislikes.

2. Promote an "Eat More Vegetables" program. Give extra credit points for students who bring vegetables in their lunches or who can tell you which vegetable they ate from the school lunch.

3. Hold an election for "The Best Vegetable." Let small groups choose and campaign for a specific vegetable. Each group should design a poster promoting their vegetable and give persuasive speeches in favor of it. When all projects have been presented, vote by secret ballot. If possible, bring in a sample of the winning veggie for all to share.

4. Have students bring in food package labels that illustrate or contain a photograph of a vegetable. Be sure that students include the portion of the label that indicates where the produce was grown. Pin the labels to a map, so that students will see where vegetables are grown.

# SPORTS

| | | | |
|---|---|---|---|
| athlete | baseball | basketball | championship |
| defense | football | goal | golf |
| hockey | offense | race | referee |
| score | skating | skiing | soccer |
| swimming | tennis | track | umpire |

1. Divide the class into groups. Have each group choose a sport. Tell the students that they are going to complete a project about their chosen sport. The project should include:

- a paragraph on the history of the sport
- a list of the basic rules
- five different articles about the sport from magazines or newspapers
- an oral presentation on the signals used by a referee or umpire in the sport, or the correct way of keeping score
- at least one written page giving information about famous athletes who have competed in the sport
- three different records that have been set by individuals or teams in the sport

2. Invite a sports reporter from the local newspaper to visit the classroom.

3. Individually or as a group, have students prepare an oral presentation in which they pretend to be a sportscaster for a national sports channel.

4. Bring in samples of the sports section from the newspaper. Have students work to create their own sports section. If possible, let them use the computer to print up headlines and stories. Another alternative is to have them cut various headlines from old newspapers, then paste them together. Students should write stories to go along with the headlines. Be sure they include articles about the sports programs in the local schools.

# ASTRONOMY

| apogee | asteroid | cluster | comet |
|---|---|---|---|
| constellation | eclipse | galaxy | meteor |
| moon | nebula | nova | orbit |
| perigee | planet | revolve | rotate |
| satellite | star | universe | zenith |

1. Have the students use index cards to make flash cards for the vocabulary words. Give each student 20 blank cards. On the lined side of each card, students should write a word and its definition. On the plain side, have students draw a picture or diagram to illustrate the word.

2. Children will then make representations of constellations. You will need a book with constellation diagrams, shoeboxes, drawing paper, pencils, black paper or paint, scissors, pushpins, glue, and tape.

Have each child remove the lid from a shoebox and line the inside of the box with black paper or paint the inside with black paint. At one end of the box, have the students cut a small, square viewing hole. Then have them cut a sheet of drawing paper the same size as the end of the shoebox. Have the students reproduce the constellation on this paper, then tape it to the inside of the shoebox opposite the viewing hole. They should use a pin to poke through the end of the box where each star is located in the constellation. Then have them remove the star pattern and put the lid on the box. Each student should write the name of the constellation on a piece of paper and glue it to the lid. By holding the shoebox up to the light and peering through the viewing hole, students will be able to see a model of the constellation.

3. Visit a planetarium or ask an astronomer to visit. Or you may know a parent who is an amateur star-gazer and is willing to make a presentation to the class.

# SEASHORE

| beach | breeze | crabs | driftwood |
|---|---|---|---|
| foam | jellyfish | ocean | otters |
| rocks | sand | sandcastle | seagulls |
| seals | seaweed | shells | starfish |
| surf | tidepools | tides | waves |

1. Let students draw pictures of the seashore. Have them include at least half of the items from the vocabulary list. Tell students to label these objects in their pictures.

2. If you have a sand play area at your school or at a nearby park, host a sandcastle-building contest. Divide the class into groups to create castles. Let the class vote on the first-prize winner.

3. Give the students a writing assignment with one of these story starters:

- I was wading through the surf at the beach when something brushed up against my ankles. I had never seen anything like it before.
- The other day I was busy digging in the sand when my shovel struck something hard. I was surprised to see a very shiny object.
- My friends and I were sunbathing on the beach. I looked over and spotted over a hundred crabs marching in a very straight line.

4. Create a mini-museum. Allow students to bring in items they have collected on trips to the seashore. Encourage them to research and correctly label each item. Also ask the class to bring in paintings, drawings, photographs, or magazine pictures of the seascapes. Set up a display in your room and invite other classes to come visit.

How to Teach Vocabulary Without Going Crazy • ©1999 Monday Morning Books

# THE NEWSPAPER

| | | | |
|---|---|---|---|
| advertisement | by-line | classifieds | columns |
| comics | editor | features | headline |
| insert | local | national | news |
| photographs | publisher | quote | reporter |
| sections | sports | weather | world |

1. Take the class to visit a local newspaper. If that is not practical, have a speaker from the newspaper visit your classroom.

2. Most newspapers have a program in which they donate free papers to area schools. Call your local paper and ask about such a program. If one is not available, ask students to bring in newspapers from home. Using the newspapers, have the students circle and identify all of the vocabulary words or sections that relate to them.

3. Create a class newspaper. Assign the various jobs and sections to different groups of students. Have some students write articles and features for the paper. Let another group obtain "advertisements" for upcoming events or cafeteria meals. Use old papers as a guideline. Then let students cut and paste their work to duplicate a newspaper format. Reproduce enough copies for your class. If possible, have enough copies made to pass out to other classrooms too.

4. In newspaper language, the morgue is a place where back issues of the paper are kept and referenced. Start building a morgue in your classroom. Ask students to cut out stories from the paper that refer to a specific subject. Try to coordinate this work with other areas of the curriculum. Fill folders with articles categorized by local, national or world news. Fill another folder with photographs. All of the information can be used as inspiration for future writing projects.

# BIRDS

| blackbird | bluebird | cardinal | chickadee |
|-----------|----------|----------|-----------|
| dove | eagle | egret | finch |
| hawk | hummingbird | lark | owl |
| partridge | pheasant | pigeon | robin |
| sparrow | starling | warbler | wren |

1. This vocabulary list is designed to enhance students' knowledge of birds and to give them alternative words to use in their writing. The list includes a variety of birds, but you may still want to include birds that are native to your area. Bring in some field guides so that students can associate each kind of bird with its picture.

2. Encourage students to watch for and identify birds in their neighborhoods. Compile a class list of all the birds the students spot.

3. Donate some nesting material to the birds. Collect the small plastic baskets used in grocery store produce departments. Tie a piece of yarn to each basket to form a handle. Have the students fill the baskets with yarn, string, twigs, cotton balls, strips of material, and dryer lint. Hang the baskets in trees or bushes. The birds will be happy to have a ready supply of nest-building materials.

4. Give students a writing assignment based on bird watching. Have them develop an adventure story or write about finding a very rare bird species.

5. Have the class make bird feeders. They can consult books in the library that describe simple bird feeders that are easy to make. Half-gallon cartons and two-liter soda bottles may be used. For example, children may cut open a large square on two sides of a container, add string for hanging, and poke a branch through the container bottom for perching. Or pinecones may be coated with peanut butter or suet, rolled in birdseed, and hung from tree branches.

How to Teach Vocabulary Without Going Crazy • ©1999 Monday Morning Books

# GEMS AND MINERALS

| | | | |
|---|---|---|---|
| agate | amber | amethyst | aquamarine |
| beryl | copper | diamond | emerald |
| garnet | gold | jade | onyx |
| opal | quartz | ruby | sapphire |
| silver | topaz | turquoise | zircon |

1. Borrow books from the library that show pictures of the gems and minerals on the vocabulary list. Take time to show each picture to the class. Then have the class, as a group, list the gems and minerals, then describe at least three characteristics of each one.

2. Both male and female middle schoolers seem to enjoy adornment, so they should enjoy designing jewelry. Encourage them to use drawing paper and colored pencils to draw necklaces, belts, lockets, bracelets, rings, earrings, tie bars, or cuff links. The students should label each gem or mineral in their sketches. Put the drawings together for a classroom jewelry design book.

3. Give students a writing assignment using one of the following titles:

- "The Pirate Treasure of Skull Island"
- "The Curse of the Pharaoh's Gem"
- "The Case of the Missing Jewel"

4. A birthstone is a gem that is a symbol of the month in which a person was born (January is garnet, May is emerald, November is topaz, and so on). We also use precious metals to describe anniversaries (for example, the 25th anniversary is silver, the 50th gold). Have students develop a list of special events and the gems they would choose to represent each one.

Examples:
first straight "A" report card—amber
eighth grade graduation—copper
high school graduation—silver
college graduation—gold

# READY TO GO

| | | | |
|---|---|---|---|
| crawl | drive | flounce | glide |
| hike | journey | march | patrol |
| ramble | ride | roam | rove |
| shuffle | slide | stride | stroll |
| swagger | tour | travel | wander |

1. Have the students write a phrase for each of the vocabulary words (hike the trail, ride a bike, march with the band, patrol the border). These phrases will help the students acquire a visual picture of the words. Then play Charades with the words. When playing the game, a successful guess need only be the correct vocabulary word. Remind students that for the purposes of this list, they should use the verb form of each word.

2. Develop an obstacle course outside. Mark off sections of the playground and sidewalks with chalk. Place a chalk line at varying spots throughout the course. At each line write a vocabulary word to designate a particular method in which the following distance must be traversed (swagger the first ten feet, shuffle for five feet, stride the next twelve).

3. Have the students design Crazy Courses. Give each student a large piece of drawing paper and crayons, markers, or colored pencils. Tell the students that they are going to make an obstacle course on paper. They must specify the method by which each section of the course is to be completed. Students should draw their projects in map-like fashion. Each section should be clearly marked with written instructions that include a vocabulary word. Allow time for each student to make an oral presentation to the class about the Crazy Course that was designed.

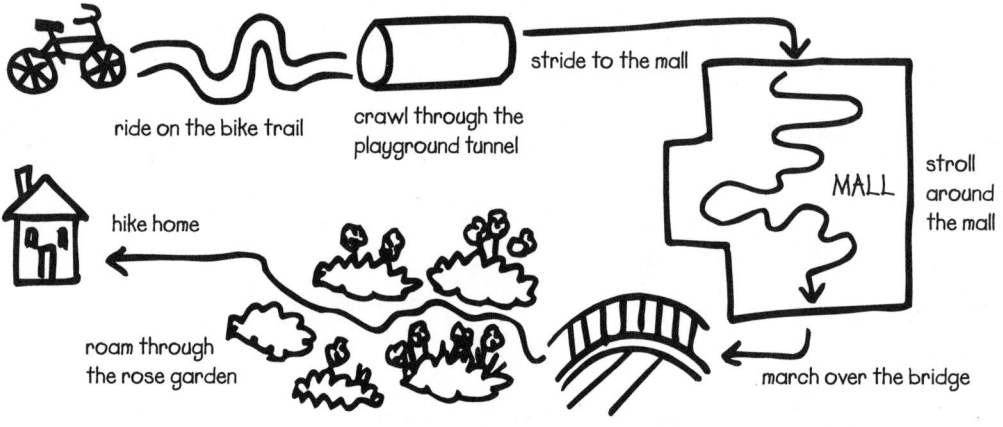

How to Teach Vocabulary Without Going Crazy • ©1999 Monday Morning Books

# BAD ATTITUDE

| | | | |
|---|---|---|---|
| awful | disgusting | dismal | dreadful |
| evil | foul | ghastly | grim |
| harsh | horrid | lousy | nasty |
| naughty | obnoxious | repulsive | rotten |
| terrible | vile | wicked | wretched |

1. Have students write a list of phrases that pairs an adjective from the list with an appropriate noun.

> **Examples:**
> rotten eggs
> foul gas
> horrid garbage

2. Give students the task of writing a really creepy story. If it is the right time of year, make it a Halloween story.

3. Ask the class to think about story and movie characters. Tell the students to match one of the vocabulary words with one character.

> **Examples:**
> wicked Witch of the West
> repulsive Jabba the Hutt
> vile Dr. No

4. Have the students write about an unpleasant experience they had. Encourage them to use as many vocabulary words as possible and underline them.

> **Example:**
> I really felt <u>awful</u>. I went to the doctor's office. The nurse came in and gave me some <u>vile</u> medicine. It was a <u>horrid</u> mixture that was supposed to be fruit flavored. It made me throw up right there. I have hated the <u>repulsive</u> flavor of artificial grape ever since that day!

# GOOD THINGS
# COME IN SMALL PACKAGES

| | | | |
|---|---|---|---|
| compact | cramped | diminutive | elfin |
| limited | little | meager | microscopic |
| miniature | minute | petite | petty |
| pinched | puny | slight | sparse |
| stunted | teeny | tiny | undersized |

1. Watch the movie <u>The Indian in the Cupboard</u>, or read the book aloud to the class.

2. Have the students look at a variety of magazine photographs. Ask them to identify small items in the pictures. Tell students to write descriptive phrases, using the vocabulary words.

> **Examples:**
> the vegetation is sparse
> there is a puny rock
> the restaurant looks cramped

3. Have the class make books entitled "Tiny Treasures." Cut a number of small drawing paper squares. Give each child 5 to 10 squares. Tell students to use one square for their book cover. Another square should be used for the first page, on which they should write the title and their name. The students should draw small pictures of some of their favorite things on the other pages. Each illustration should have a title written above it that uses one of the vocabulary words.

> **Examples:**
> elfin hamster
> diminutive ballerina
> limited-edition baseball card

4. Give the class a writing assignment using this story starter:

> I was reading a book when I heard a strange knocking at the door. I went to investigate and was very surprised to discover a miniature _____ right outside my door!

How to Teach Vocabulary Without Going Crazy • ©1999 Monday Morning Books

# IT IS BETTER TO GIVE THAN TO RECEIVE

| accept | award | bestow | contribute |
|---|---|---|---|
| derive | dispense | donate | endow |
| entrust | furnish | gain | grant |
| inherit | issue | obtain | pocket |
| present | provide | secure | supply |

1. Go over the vocabulary words in class. Point out that some of the words may be used as nouns, but when working with this list, the verb form and definition should be used. Have the students make two columns on their papers, one headed "Give" and one labeled "Receive." The students are to look up the definition of each word and place it in the correct column.

2. Read "The Gift of the Magi" by O. Henry.

3. Begin a class service project. Collect canned goods or personal hygiene items and donate them to a local food bank or homeless shelter. During cold weather, you might collect new and slightly used socks, hats, and mittens to give to the needy.

4. Let each student come up with a "Wacky Award" to present to another student. Write each student's name on a slip of paper and place the slips in a basket. Have each child draw the name of a classmate. Be sure that you discuss with the class which types of awards are appropriate. Stress to the class that no feelings are to be hurt. The awards should be positive and lighthearted. Give students drawing paper so that they may design certificates for the awards.

When it is time to make the presentations, discuss the type of vocabulary the students must use during the ceremony. When handing out an award, for example, the student should say: "I bestow the title of Best Skateboarder to _____." Or, "I present this award for Most Stylish Earrings to _____." As students accept their award, they must also use a vocabulary word: "I humbly accept this wonderful award" or "I was able to obtain this honor through a lot of hard work."

5. Give the class a writing assignment that focuses on a time when it was definitely better to give than to receive.

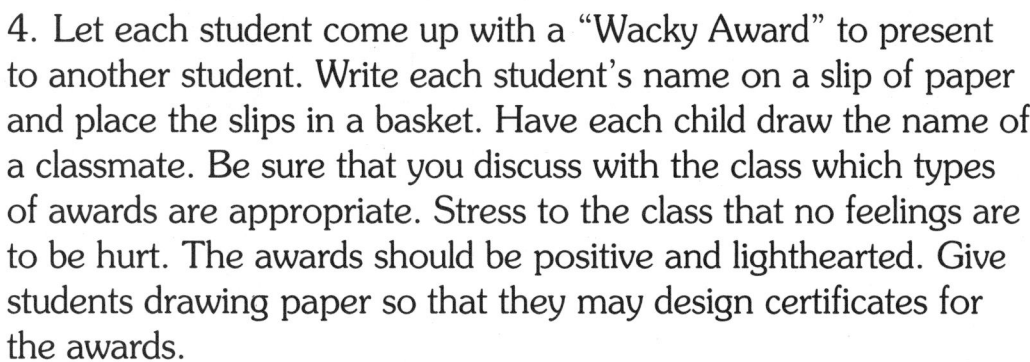

# MORE THAN JUST PRETTY

| | | | |
|---|---|---|---|
| attractive | beautiful | charming | dazzling |
| delicate | divine | elegant | enchanting |
| exquisite | glorious | gorgeous | handsome |
| lovely | radiant | ravishing | resplendent |
| sparkling | splendid | stunning | sublime |

1. Have students cut out magazine pictures of scenery or objects that they feel could be described by one of the vocabulary words. Create a large collage using the pictures.

2. Read a version of "The Ugly Duckling" to the class. Then give students this writing assignment: Write a story about an "ugly duckling" in an otherwise perfect world. Include as many vocabulary words as possible.

3. Ask the class to write analogies using the vocabulary words (see p. 66).

4. Bring a large variety of fairy tale books to the classroom. Have the students search through the tales in pairs to find examples of the vocabulary words. Once they find a word, tell the students to write down a sentence that contains it as well as the title of the fairy tale in which it was found. Encourage students to find other words that could be added to this vocabulary list.

5. Have a class discussion on the meaning of some of these quotes:

> *Beauty and Truth, though never found, are worthy to be sought.*
> —Robert Buchanan
> *The sublime and the ridiculous are often so nearly related, that it is difficult to class them separately.*
> —Thomas Paine
> *The young are beautiful, but the old are more beautiful than the young.*
> —Walt Whitman
> *Beauty is altogether in the eye of the beholder.*
> —Lew Wallace
> *Everything has its beauty, but not everyone sees it.*
> —Confucius

 How to Teach Vocabulary Without Going Crazy • ©1999 Monday Morning Books

# MAKE IT BETTER

| | | | |
|---|---|---|---|
| **assemble** | **build** | **compose** | **construct** |
| **craft** | **create** | **design** | **develop** |
| **devise** | **draft** | **fashion** | **form** |
| **invent** | **manufacture** | **mold** | **produce** |
| **sculpt** | **sew** | **weave** | **write** |

1. Adapt the activity called "What's in a Name?" (see p. 55). Have the children add a phrase to each name that uses the verb form of the vocabulary words.

> **Examples:**
> Carrie A. Tune has composed a symphony.
> Paige Turner is going to write a book about carousels.
> Ima Stitch can sew fabulous monograms on anything.

2. Have students choose a word and develop a project to go along with that word. For example, they may devise a plan to sew a pillow, build a castle, weave a basket, compose a song, mold a clay animal, produce a skit, assemble a model, draft a plan for a house, invent a cool new item, craft a picture frame from shells. Hold an Experience Fair during which students display and describe their ventures.

3. Play the game "What's My Line?" To play, students need to take one of the vocabulary words and turn it into a statement about a profession.

> **Examples:**
> I manufacture snowboards.
> I develop new ice cream flavors.
> My job is to assemble computers.
> I fashion clothes from recycled materials.

To play the game, the contestant comes to the front of the room. A judge is chosen to sit with the contestant to be sure all answers are truthful and to help clear up any confusion. The class may ask up to 20 questions that can be answered with a "yes" or "no" to determine the contestant's profession.

# PICTURESQUE SPEECH

## Figurative Language I (Metaphors)

a bridge over troubled waters

apple of one's eye

busy as a bee

butterflies in the stomach

jump on the bandwagon

just spinning your wheels

looking at the world through rose-colored glasses

mad as a hornet

paint the town red

put your foot in your mouth

raining cats and dogs

roll out the red carpet

straight from the horse's mouth

tough as nails

walking on air

1. Discuss the meanings of the phrases with your students. Then tell the class that they are going to write "If. . . then . . . " statements. These statements are comprised of two phrases: the first indicates a cause, and the second states an effect. In each of the statements the effect should include one of the metaphors.

> **Examples:**
> If Bryce comes home from college this weekend, then we will roll out the red carpet.
> If Shaun wins the music contest, then he will be walking on air.

2. Assign students the task of finding a one-word synonym that aptly corresponds to each of the figurative language phrases. Allow students to use the dictionary and the thesaurus for help. Have each student create a matching worksheet. On the left side of the paper they should write each phrase. On the right side, in a different order, they should write each one-word synonym. After the worksheets are completed, have the students trade papers with a partner and try to correctly match the pairs.

3. By middle school most students are familiar with writing poetry. If you feel your class needs a review, though, spend some time reading samples and discussing the formats of various poems. Then tell the students that they are going to create simple poems that include figurative phrases. Reluctant writers may need a specific formula to follow, but other students should be allowed a free choice of format. Students should write four-line poems following either the AABB or ABAB rhyme pattern.

**Example of AABB rhyme scheme:**
I wanted to go looking for frogs,
But it started to rain cats and dogs.
I felt this was really bad luck,
Now I'm swimming around like a duck.

**Example of ABAB rhyme scheme:**
Dad said I was too young to drive,
But I took the car just to see.
I'm lucky to still be alive;
Dad's mad as a hornet would be!

# Figurative Language II

a little bird told me

an ax to grind

barking up the wrong tree

bend over backwards to help

bury the hatchet

don't blow your top

know the ropes

lay all the cards on the table

march to a different drummer

put your two cents in

running on empty

sharp as a tack

that will happen when pigs fly

the sky's the limit

until the cows come home

a little bird told me

KNOW THE ROPES

the sky's the limit

UNTIL THE COWS COME HOME

march to a different drummer

1. Play Charades using the figurative phrases. Write each phrase on a slip of paper. Then divide the class into teams, or just let the whole class guess as a student acts out the phrase.

2. Have students copy down the phrases. Then tell them to ask family members what the metaphors mean. Have students write a brief definition for each of the figurative language phrases. Take some class time to let students present the meanings they have discovered. Discuss why some of the meanings may be different.

3. Use the metaphors as story starters. Tell students to choose one of the phrases for their title and to develop a corresponding story.

4. Have students try writing a story that uses as many of the figurative language phrases as possible.

5. Have students scan for a paragraph in a current reading selection in which one of the vocabulary phrases could be reasonably inserted. Have students rewrite the paragraph incorporating the phrase.

# Figurative Language III

a horse of a different color

chip off the old block

eyes in the back of one's head

fly off the handle

game of cat and mouse

has a green thumb

head in the clouds

his elevator doesn't go all the way to the top floor

once in a blue moon

pot calling the kettle black

spill the beans

steal someone else's thunder

steam coming out of one's ears

talk your ear off

that's just the tip of the iceberg

1. Have students write two sentences for each figurative language phrase. One sentence should include the metaphor. The other sentence should be written in a way that explains the phrase.

Examples:
Lisa can sure talk your ear off.
Lisa really enjoys talking a lot.

Paul takes a day off only once in a blue moon.
Paul very rarely takes a day off from work.

The teacher seems to have eyes in the back of her head.
The teacher always seems to know what is going on, even if she is turned away from us.

eyes in the back of one's head

FLY OFF THE HANDLE

head in the clouds

talk your ear off

game of cat and mouse

spill the beans

2. Instruct the students to choose three to five of the figurative language phrases. Using markers, pens, colored pencils, and drawing paper, they should create cartoon versions of the metaphors. Have students illustrate what each phrase seems to be saying, not what it actually means. For example, an illustration of "game of cat and mouse" would show a cat and a mouse playing.

3. Create a class compilation of "Familyisms"—phrases a family or friend uses over and over. First let the students share the regularly used phrases in class; be sure to remind students that the language must be school appropriate. Then write the phrases on a large piece of newsprint, or use index cards to create a file. Encourage students to use the phrases occasionally in their writing or speech.

steam coming out of his ears

has a green thumb

# Proverbs I

Short explanations of often-used proverbs are provided for teacher reference on the next several pages. When you introduce the proverbs to the students, don't include the explanations. Allow time for discussion and let the class draw their own conclusions about the meanings of these sayings.

two heads are better than one

**A bird in hand is worth two in the bush.** It is usually better to take advantage of an opportunity in the present, rather than to hold out for the possibility of something better.

**A watched pot never boils.** When we are excited and looking forward to something, time always seems to pass slowly.

**Better bend than break.** Sometimes it is better to compromise than get into a conflict that you will later regret.

**Clothes do not make the man.** The outward appearance of a person does not always give a clear indication of the personality inside.

Don't put all your eggs in one basket.

**Cross that bridge when you come to it.** Don't worry needlessly about something that may not even occur. Take care of problems one at a time.

**Don't change horses in midstream.** Choose the right moment to make changes. Finish what you have started.

**Don't put all your eggs in one basket.** Be sure you have alternative ways of handling situations.

**Don't put the cart before the horse.** Deal with things in a logical order. Very similar to "Cross that bridge when you come to it."

**Every cloud has a silver lining.** Even in times of trouble, there is usually something good that can be made of a bad situation.

**Every oak must be an acorn.** Everything has a small beginning. Don't get discouraged.

**Love is blind.** People who love one another do not focus on the other person's faults.

**Many hands make light work.** When everyone pitches in to help, the work will soon get done.

**The early bird catches the worm.** The person with a lot of enthusiasm and willingness to work will achieve his or her goals.

**Two heads are better than one.** Often two people working together are able to resolve a situation that a person alone would be unable to do.

**United we stand, divided we fall.** Unity is strength. If group members fight among themselves, they will not reach their goal.

1. Ask each student to choose one proverb. Have the students ask at least five people to explain the meaning of the proverb. Be sure that the children interview people in different age groups. Students should write up the answers they received. Take some time for sharing the results in small-group discussions.

2. Remind students that fables are stories that end with a moral or message. Often these morals are familiar proverbs. If you wish, begin by reading a few fables to the class. Then divide the class into small groups. Have each group come up with and present a short skit that relates to and concludes with a proverb. The skits may be presented in a very short amount of time or you may want to make a bigger production of the project. The project could be expanded by having students develop costumes, props, and scenery.

3. Provide drawing paper, markers, colored pencils, and crayons. Let students have fun drawing cartoon sketches that illustrate the concrete meaning of three to five of the proverbs.

# Proverbs II

**Absence makes the heart grow fonder.** People often do not realize how much they care for another until they are apart.

**Actions speak louder than words.** What you do is much more important than what you say you will do.

**All good things must come to an end.** Pleasure cannot go on forever; all things change.

**Better safe than sorry.** It is better to go slowly and thoughtfully than to rush into a situation.

**Easier said than done.** It is easier to talk about your goals than to accomplish them.

**Enough is as good as a feast.** If your needs are fulfilled, do not spend a lot of time wishing for more.

**If a thing is worth doing it is worth doing well.** Any task that is worthy of your attention is worthy of your best effort.

**Let bygones be bygones.** Forgive and forget, don't dwell on the past.

**Let sleeping dogs lie.** Don't stir up unnecessary trouble.

**Necessity is the mother of invention.** The need to solve a problem often leads to the birth of a new idea.

**Once bitten, twice shy.** If you have had an unpleasant experience you will be very anxious to avoid repeating it.

**People who live in glass houses shouldn't throw stones.** Those whose own behavior is open to criticism should not criticize others.

**Rome was not built in a day.** Important tasks require a lot of hard work and patience.

**To err is human.** Everyone makes mistakes.

**Where there is a will there is a way.** If you are determined to accomplish a goal you will find a means to succeed.

1. Take some time to discuss each proverb. Do not give the explanations immediately and remain open-minded. Let the class determine the meanings. Often students will come up with a very logical and appropriate concept that is somewhat different than the traditional meaning.

2. Divide the class into small groups. Let the students discuss and tell stories about experiences in their lives that a proverb might apply to. Before having students speak, you may want to review some story telling techniques with the class (for example, speak clearly and loud enough for all to hear; remember to relate events in the order in which they occurred; stay with the subject; do not let your story wander off the track). Encourage all students to participate. Strongly remind the class that classmates should not be ridiculed or teased about an experience they are willing to share.

3. Prepare role playing cards for the students to work with in class or to be given as an assignment. Each card should contain a brief description of an event or situation. Have the students read aloud a description and then determine a proverb that would apply.

> **Example:**
> **Event—**Jackie fell and broke her leg while ice skating. It took a very long time for her to recover. When she was better, her friends invited her to go skating. Jackie refused. No matter how much coaxing her friends did, she still would not put on a pair of skates.
> **Proverb—**Once bitten, twice shy.

4. Before class, cut bookmark size strips of poster board. Supply students with stickers, markers, crayons, or colored pencils. Tell students that they are going to make bookmarks. Have them choose their favorite proverb and write it on the strip of poster board. Then have them decorate the strip to make an attractive bookmark. The bookmarks may be given to friends, family, or younger students as gifts. You may wish to let students create one bookmark for a gift and another for themselves.

# Proverbs III

**A good name is sooner lost than won.** It takes a long time to build up a good reputation, but it can be quickly lost by one instance of bad behavior.

**All that glitters is not gold.** Do not be fooled by outward appearances. A lovely exterior does not assure a beautiful interior.

**Any port in a storm.** In times of trouble, any relief is better than none at all.

**Courtesy costs nothing.** Everyone is capable of being polite without any cost to themselves.

**Don't count your chickens before they are hatched.** Do not rely too heavily on a given situation; it may change or not be what you expected.

**Don't cut off your nose to spite your face.** Don't do something in anger now that will cause you greater problems later.

**Haste makes waste.** Hurrying through a task usually means it will have to be redone, wasting time and resources.

**Hope springs eternal.** It is human nature to look ahead to better times.

**Learn to walk before you run.** A skill is best learned one step at a time. Do not become discouraged.

**Look before you leap.** Analyze a situation before charging ahead. This includes thinking before you speak.

**One good turn deserves another.** If someone has shown you a kindness, you should do something nice in return.

**Speech is silver, silence is golden.** Gold is more precious than silver. There are times when it is better to be silent than to speak out.

**The darkest hour is before the dawn.** Things will often seem to be at their very worst just before they start to improve.

**Time and tide wait for no man.** We cannot stop time from passing or the tide from flowing. If an opportunity presents itself you should act upon it.

**Two wrongs don't make a right.** Taking revenge on someone will not improve a bad situation.

1. Discuss the proverbs and their meanings with the class. You may wish to do this in small groups first and then have each group report their conclusions to the entire class. Point out to the class that groups may have varying impressions about what the proverbs are trying to say. Be sure to set an example by being flexible in your acceptance of different ideas.

2. Ask students to think about how these proverbs may apply to their own lives. Provide large sheets of drawing paper or poster board. Have each student use markers, crayons, or colored pencils to design a poster that illustrates one of the proverbs. You may wish to have magazines available for students to cut out pictures to add to their posters. Consider displaying the posters when parents will be visiting; they make great conversation starters.

3. Have students use one of the proverbs as a story starter. The proverb may be used as the title of the story or as the conclusion. Begin by reading a few of Aesop's Fables to the class for inspiration; they are good examples of stories that conclude with a moral and illustrate morals on which many of our proverbs are based.

4. Have the students make Proverb Pockets:

**Materials:**
Blue construction paper, white or yellow crayons, scissors, glue, strips of white paper

**Preparation:**
Cut enough pieces of construction paper in half so that *every* student receives two pieces. Cut enough white paper strips so that each student receives five strips.

**Procedure:**
Have the children use one piece of blue paper for the base. From the other blue paper, have them cut a large pentagon shape that looks like a pocket. Have them put glue on three edges of this shape and attach it to the base paper, leaving the top edge unglued to form the pocket. Using white or yellow crayon, have students add little dashes to make the pocket look like it has been stitched on. Some children may want to add extra stitching and details so that their pockets resemble their favorite brand of jeans. When the pockets are ready, tell students to choose five proverbs that they connect with or that have meaning for them. Have them write one proverb on each strip of white paper and place the strips in their Proverb Pocket.

# WORD STRUCTURE

## Roots

Roots and base words are often confused, but both are important building blocks of language. It is important for students to understand the difference between the two.

Elementary students work with base words from the very beginning. Base words are able to stand alone: for example, play. A prefix may be added to the base word: replay. A suffix may be added to the base word: played. Both a prefix and a suffix may be attached to the base word: replayed.

Roots are not actually words that are able to stand alone. They consist of a group of letters that have a meaning, and most have a Greek or Latin origin. The group of letters acts as a building block to form the foundation of a complete word. For example, therm, a Greek root meaning heat, gives us the word thermometer.

Latin roots dominate our language. Sometimes they are quite obvious: the root <u>ped</u>, meaning <u>foot</u>, gives us <u>pedal</u>, which is a lever operated by the foot. Other times roots are less obvious: the root <u>spic</u>, meaning to see, gives us <u>conspicuous</u>, meaning easy to see or perceive.

Other roots take even more imagination to make the connection between origin and meaning. Consider <u>gest</u>, a root meaning <u>carry</u>. The word <u>congestion</u> means carried or collected into a mass.

Fourth graders should continue to work with base words and learn the meanings of prefixes and suffixes. Near the end of sixth grade, root words may be brought in as an enrichment unit. The concept of roots should be seriously addressed in seventh grade. By the end of eighth grade some students may be veritable wizards at root detection.

The next several activities focus on roots. A number of them provide lists of roots and specific exercises that correlate with them. Pick and choose the lessons that you feel will be most beneficial to your class.

# Root Trees

## Materials:
Drawing paper; brown, green, and red colored pencils or markers; list of vocabulary words or dictionaries

## Activity:
1. Tell the class that they are going to "grow" root trees for specific roots and their word derivatives.

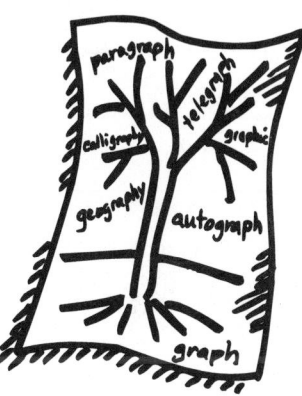

2. Give each student a piece of drawing paper. Have each student draw a simple bare tree shape using a brown marker. Be sure the trees include roots and several branches.

3. Have the students use a red marker to write a root by the tree roots. Have them use a green marker to write all the words they can think of that contain the root in the bare branches.

4. Encourage students to scan the dictionary for more words to place on their trees. If the trees are saved in a folder, additional word derivatives can be added as they are discovered throughout the year.

# Word Arithmetic

**Materials:**
Pencils and paper

**Activity:**
1. Remind students about number sentences and equations used in math. Write a few examples on the board, for example:

> 4 + 2 + 8 = 14          7 + (6 x 3) - 5 = 20
> 8 - 6 + (12 - 2) + 4 = 16

2. Show students how compound words can be put together in much the same manner:

> mail + box = mailbox          gold + fish = goldfish
> snow + ball = snowball

3. Progress to base words with a prefix and a suffix:

> un + end + ing = unending
> re + start + ed = restarted

4. Have students examine the vocabulary list of words and identify the root in each. They should then create a word arithmetic equation for each word. It is helpful to specify the manner in which the roots are to be identified, for example, by circling, underlining, or boxing the various parts of the equation.

> con + duc + ive = conducive
> dis + pos + able = disposable

**118**

# Digging for Roots

**Materials:**
Paper and pencils, dictionaries, vocabulary journals, drawing paper

**Activity:**
1. Divide the class into small groups or partners. Give each group a specific root, its meaning, and an example of a word derived from that root.

2. Tell the groups they have 15 minutes (or whatever time limit is desired) to find as many words containing that root as possible.

3. Give each group a piece of drawing paper. Let the students design a poster that highlights the root and includes all of the words they have discovered.

> Here are some common roots that may be used with this activity:
> **auto**—self (autograph, autobiography)
> **bio**—life (biology, biopsy)
> **loc**—place (location, local)
> **magni**—great (magnify, magnitude)
> **port**—carry (transport, portable)
> **script**—write (scripture, transcript)
> **sist**—stand or set (consist, resist)
> **tele**—distance (telephone, telemetry)
> **therm**—heat (thermal, thermostat)
> **voc**—voice (vocabulary, vocal)

# The Roots dou and du—Meaning "Two"

| | | | |
|---|---|---|---|
| deuce | double | doubly | doubt |
| doubter | doubtful | doubtfully | doubting |
| dual | dualism | dubious | dubiously |
| duel | dueling | duet | duplicate |
| duplication | duplicator | duplicity | indubitably |

1. Have the students work in pairs.

2. Tell the children to play the Memory game using this list (see p. 33).

3. Have them use each word or form of a word two times in a sentence.

> **Examples:**
> With deuces wild, a deuce beats a king.
> To duplicate the formula, we will need a duplicating machine.

4. Have each student write simple doublet sentences for at least five vocabulary words. A doublet makes sense whether you read it forwards or backwards.

> **Examples:**
> Dubious Jenn made tales unbelievable.
> Unbelievable tales made Jenn dubious.
>
> Dueling boys stopped Chris.
> Chris stopped boys dueling.
>
> Together, Lisa and Leslie sang duets.
> "Duets," sang Leslie and Lisa together.

Doublets are tough, so encourage the students to use punctuation to help.

How to Teach Vocabulary Without Going Crazy • ©1999 Monday Morning Books

# The Roots graph and gram—
# Meaning "Write"

| | | | |
|---|---|---|---|
| anagram | autobiography | autograph | bibliography |
| biography | calligraphy | choreographer | cryptography |
| diagram | geography | geographical | grammar |
| graphic | graphically | monogram | paragraph |
| photograph | photographer | telegraph | topographic |

1. Let students design some cryptography. Have them develop a code that replaces each letter of the alphabet with a number or another letter. Then have them write each vocabulary word in code and give the words to a friend to decode.

2. Give students the following project for an assignment:

- Write your <u>autobiography</u>.
- Use fancy <u>calligraphy</u> to write on the title page.
- Add a <u>graphic</u> to your cover page.
- Be sure you use <u>paragraphs</u> in your writing.
- Include a <u>photograph.</u>
- Check your writing for proper <u>grammar</u>.
- Make a <u>topographic</u> map of the state where you were born.
- At the end of your project, write your <u>monogram</u>.

3. Have students make <u>anagrams</u>, or scramble the letters of each of the vocabulary words. Have them trade with a friend and try to unscramble each other's words.

4. Give this assignment to your students:

Write a short <u>biography</u> about a <u>choreographer</u>, the inventor of the <u>telegraph</u>, a famous <u>photographer</u>, or a <u>graphic</u> artist.

# The Root pos—Meaning "To Put" or "Set"

| | | | |
|---|---|---|---|
| compose | composer | composite | composure |
| deposit | disposable | dispose | expose |
| impose | juxtapose | oppose | pose |
| position | postpone | posture | propose |
| purpose | superimpose | suppose | transpose |

1. Have the students make <u>composite</u>, <u>superimposed</u> pictures. Give the students a wide variety of magazine pictures. Have them choose one photograph as the base. Then have them cut out singular items from other photographs and glue these to the base photograph to form the <u>composite.</u>

2. Have students write a report about a famous <u>composer</u>.

3. Hold a debate. In the debate format, a <u>position</u> is supported by one group of debaters. Another group <u>oppose</u>s the position. Be sure that students clearly state the <u>purpose</u> of each argument.

Divide the class into small groups. Then pair up the groups, one a supporting team and one an opposing team. Assign each pair a topic to be debated. Give students time to develop their reasons and supporting arguments.

During the actual debate, the supporting (affirmative) team should present its arguments first. This should be limited to about 5–8 minutes. Next, the opposing (negative) side has its chance to speak for 5–8 minutes. The affirmative team then has 2–3 minutes to restate its position or rebut the opposing team's statements. Finally, the negative team makes its rebuttal statements.

Fast-food restaurants should serve lunches in school cafeterias.

Here are some possible topics:
- Public school students should wear uniforms.
- The government should regulate Internet Web sites.
- Television should have stricter guidelines for children's programs.
- All sports should have salary caps for players.
- Fast-food restaurants should serve lunches in school cafeterias.

# The Roots spec and spic—Meaning "To see" and "Kind or Type"

| | | | |
|---|---|---|---|
| aspect | conspicuous | disrespect | expect |
| expectation | inspect | inspector | perspective |
| prospect | respect | respectful | special |
| species | specify | specimen | spectacular |
| spectator | suspect | suspicion | unexpected |

1. Have students make two columns on their papers. Have them label one column "to see" and the other "kind or type." Tell students to look up each vocabulary word in the dictionary. Have them determine which category each word falls into and write the word under the appropriate heading.

2. Have the students create Root Trees for the vocabulary words (see p. 117).

3. Have students compose a rap song about <u>respect</u>. Encourage them to use as many vocabulary words as possible in the song.

4. Go over the vocabulary words with your class. Point out that many of the words are often found in mystery stories. Give the class the assignment of writing a short mystery. Tell them to include at least half of the words from the list.

5. Divide the class into small discussion groups. Give each group one of the following prompts to discuss:

How <u>disrespect</u> can lead to serious problems

- An occasion when my <u>expectations</u> were not met
- A time my <u>perspective</u> changed
- How I plan to develop <u>prospects</u> for my future
- A time when my <u>suspicions</u> led to <u>unexpected</u> results
- The person I most <u>respect</u>
- Times when it is best to <u>specify</u> a preference
- How <u>disrespect</u> can lead to serious problems

Have each group choose a spokesperson to share the group's discussion experience or point of view with the class.

# The Roots ced, cede, ceed, and cess— Meaning "Move, go along, or yield"

| | | | |
|---|---|---|---|
| access | accessible | accessorize | accessory |
| concede | exceed | exceeding | procedure |
| proceed | proceeding | process | recede |
| recess | recessive | secede | secession |
| succeed | succeeding | success | successful |

1. Give students the task of writing each vocabulary word and then using a light-colored marker to highlight its root.

2. Have students write each word and its definition. Have them review this information by playing Concentration (see p. 31).

3. Have the students give a speech on the <u>procedure</u> for becoming <u>successful</u> at a certain <u>process.</u> Give students time to work on their speeches. Help students to outline what they intend to say so that they do not just read the speech; they may want to write down the steps of the process and use this for their outline. Encourage students to use props with their speeches. Award bonus points for *every* vocabulary word that is used in a speech.

How to bargain-shop at the mall ...

Here are a few suggestions for topics:
• How to wrap a present
• The best way to train a dog to fetch
• How to cook a pizza
• The process of using search engines on the Internet
• How to bargain-shop at the mall
• The best way to train for a specific sport
• Tips for the successful babysitter
• The procedure used to secure a top score on a certain video game
• How to mow the lawn
• The best way to earn big tips as a newspaper carrier

How to Teach Vocabulary Without Going Crazy • ©1999 Monday Morning Books

# The Root duc—Meaning "Lead or bring to view"

| | | | |
|---|---|---|---|
| aqueduct | conduct | conduction | conductor |
| deduct | deductible | deduction | duct |
| educate | education | educator | introduce |
| introduction | produce | production | reduce |
| reduced | reproduce | reproduction | viaduct |

1. Host a scavenger hunt. Bring in old newspapers and magazines. Let students hunt through these to find as many vocabulary words as possible. Students should cut out each word as it is found and glue the words to a piece of newsprint to create a class collage.

2. Tell students to create Word Arithmetic problems for each vocabulary word (see p. 118). Following each equation, they should write the definition of the word.

3. Hold a "DUC Fair" in your room. Post the list of activities below for students to choose from or set up a station for each endeavor.

- Use **deduction** to solve logic problems. (Duplicate enough copies of logic problems to have each student get one.)
- **Reproduce** a simple drawing. (Provide drawing paper and colored pencils. Give students a picture to reproduce; greeting card illustrations work well.)
- **Conduct** an experiment. (Make supplies available for a simple experiment, such as which items sink or float or the best design for a paper airplane.)
- **Produce** a small sculpture. (Supply <u>duct</u> tape, cardboard, craft sticks, and other items.)
- Write an **introduction**. (Tell students to pretend their favorite sports or entertainment personality will be visiting the class. Have them write the introduction they would use to introduce the person to the class.)

# Initialisms and Acronyms

Our lives are bombarded daily with a wide assortment of "alphabet soup." Often we use these initials and acronyms without even realizing their meanings. An acronym is a word formed by the first or first few letters of words in a phrase or name, such as RAM. An initialism is similar to an acronym, but each initial is pronounced individually and does not form a word, such as CIA.

| | |
|---|---|
| **CIA** | Central Intelligence Agency |
| **DARE** | Drug Awareness and Resistance Education |
| **FAA** | Federal Aviation Administration |
| **FBI** | Federal Bureau of Investigation |
| **FCC** | Federal Communications Commission |
| **FDA** | Food and Drug Administration |
| **FDIC** | Federal Deposit Insurance Corporation |
| **IRS** | Internal Revenue Service |
| **laser** | light amplification by stimulated emission of radiation |
| **NASA** | National Aeronautics and Space Administration |
| **NATO** | North Atlantic Treaty Organization |
| **NBA** | National Basketball Association |
| **NFL** | National Football League |
| **radar** | radio detecting and ranging |
| **RAM** | random access memory |
| **ROM** | read only memory |
| **SADD** | Students Against Drunk Driving |
| **scuba** | self-contained underwater breathing apparatus |
| **sonar** | sound navigation ranging |
| **VISTA** | Volunteers in Service to America |

1. As a class, divide the list into acronyms and initialisms. Point out that sometimes only the first letter of each main word is used. Discuss with the students whether they have heard any of the acronyms or initialisms and, if so, in what context they were used.

2. Let students create their own acronyms and crazy organizations. Encourage students to match the word used as an acronym with the type of organization it represents.

> **Examples:**
> COOKIE  Culinary Organization of Kitchen's Interesting Edibles
> SWAMP  Students Working Against Muddy Places
> HOPPER  Helping Our Precious Pets and Energetic Rabbits
> DUMB  Devotees of Useless, Meaningless Busywork

3. Start a class collage or poster. On a large piece of paper, write the heading "Initialisms and Acronyms." Have students bring in examples of these that they find in newspapers or magazines. Allow them to write in an acronym that they learned from a source they could not bring to school.

4. Have students take their own initials and develop an organization to match. Remind them that the organization's name should be school appropriate. Encourage the children to have fun. They may want to create additional names using relatives' or friends' initials.

> **Examples:**
> BEC British Espionage Command
> SAC Snake Acrobat Club
> JLM Junior League of Magicians
> BJM Bungee Jumping Maniacs

If desired, allow students to design a logo for their organizations. You may even want to carry this activity a step further and assign a writing project in which students describe the activities of their organizations.

# About the Author

Cheryl L. Callighan earned her degree from Illinois State University. She has graduate credits from Concordia and Northern Illinois University. During 20 years of teaching she has worked with children in a wide range of grade levels. She has been director and curriculum author for children's summer programs in several communities. Cheryl currently works with fifth and sixth graders in De Kalb, Illinois.